Contents

Introduction

↓

SERMON
is 8|28

OLD TESTAMENT CHALLENGE 4

PURSUING **SPIRITUAL** AUTHENTICITY

ESTHER

JONAH

OTC

OLD TESTAMENT
CHALLENGE 4

PURSUING SPIRITUAL AUTHENTICITY

LIFE-CHANGING WORDS FROM THE PROPHETS

JOHN ORTBERG
WITH KEVIN & SHERRY HARNEY

ZONDERVAN™
GRAND RAPIDS, MICHIGAN 49530 USA

WILLOW
Willow Creek Resources

We want to hear from you. Please send your comments about this book to us in care of zreview@zondervan.com. Thank you.

ZONDERVAN™

Old Testament Challenge: Pursuing Spiritual Authenticity — Discussion Guide
Copyright © 2004 by Willow Creek Association

Requests for information should be addressed to:

Zondervan, *Grand Rapids, Michigan 49530*

ISBN 0-310-25144-3

Interior design by Sharon VanLoozenoord

Interior composition by Tracey Moran

Printed in the United States of America

04 05 06 07 08 09 /❖ DC/ 10 9 8 7 6 5 4 3 2 1

Introduction

The words of the Old Testament prophets cut through the millennia, grab us by our shoulders, and shake us from our slumber. Like a bucket of ice-cold water, they pour over us and shock us with the message that God is alive, God still speaks, and he is calling us to radically authentic lives. The words of the prophets address us right where we live and call us to new and fresh places of spiritual growth.

In this discussion guide we hear many voices:

- Elijah gives us an example of holding steady in a world that has lots of ups and downs.
- Elisha and his mentor Elijah model the practice of passing the torch of a spiritual legacy to the next generation.
- Amos cries out and warns us that God's perfect justice becomes the measuring line for our lives. God himself cares about justice and wants us to care just as much.
- Isaiah shows us what authentic worship and obedience look like, and through his example we are invited into a deeper place of intimacy with God.
- Hezekiah learns that radical trust is the only way to follow God, even when everyone else gives in to fear. His life shows us how to walk in new levels of trust in God.
- Micah calls us to do justice, love kindness, and walk humbly with God in a world that knows little of these things.
- Jeremiah's example helps us see that even when we face painful and hard times, we can still hold onto God and serve him.

God speaks through his prophets to let us know that his plan for us is to live in hope. Even when times are difficult and our eyes cannot see what lies ahead, we can trust that God has a plan that is good, right, and hope-filled!

Does God really still speak to his people? Can we hear his voice and follow his leading in a way that will bring transformation to our lives? Do the words of God connect in a way that will penetrate the human heart and shape us into all we hope and dream we can become? The answer is a crystal clear *Yes!*

OTC

The words of the prophets trumpet over the centuries and call us to authentic spiritual lives. God longs for each of us to see his character mirrored in us. This small group study takes you through the prophets' words and unveils truths that will help you enter new levels of spiritual maturity.

Elijah: Holding Steady in a Roller Coaster World

SESSION 1: 1 KINGS 17:7–24; 18:16–19:18

Introduction

Ancient Israel had many kings, and every one of them is said to have done evil in the eyes of God. But when Omri comes along, he is the worst of all—that is, until his son Ahab takes the throne! Ahab takes evil to new heights and the people of Israel to new depths of sin. The writer of 1 Kings 16:30–33 puts it this way:

> *Ahab son of Omri did more evil in the eyes of the LORD than any of those before him. He not only considered it trivial to commit the sins of Jeroboam son of Nebat, but he also married Jezebel daughter of Ethbaal king of the Sidonians, and began to serve Baal and worship him. He set up an altar for Baal in the temple of Baal that he built in Samaria. Ahab also made an Asherah pole and did more to provoke the LORD, the God of Israel, to anger than did all the kings of Israel before him.*

Ahab marries a pagan wife from Sidon named Jezebel, who becomes famous for her hatred of God and his prophets. Ahab puts her in charge of Israel's religion, and her express agenda is to destroy the worship of Yahweh in all the land of Israel and to replace the one true God with her god, Baal. Among other things, Jezebel seeks to systematically kill all of God's prophets.

The prophet Elijah begins his ministry when Ahab and Jezebel are on the throne. This is clearly not a popular time to go into the ministry of Yahweh in the northern kingdom. It would be like declaring you wanted to be a pastor in Communist Russia in the 1960s or deciding to become a Jewish rabbi in Germany when Hitler was in power. But God calls Elijah to step into his ministry in a time of unparalleled tension, apostasy, and danger. This roller coaster time demands a prophet who is ready to hold on and follow God through the highs and lows of doing ministry in such a climate.

Looking at Life

1 What are some possible consequences for a nation when their leaders are corrupt and evil?

Give some modern-day examples where God calls his people to stand up and speak even though what they say may not be received well.

Learning from the Word
Read: 1 Kings 17:7–24

RECKLESS GENEROSITY

The widow of Zarephath in this story is recklessly generous. She gives the last of what she has to Elijah. We should all pause occasionally and ask if we are living with that kind of generous spirit. Maybe we have a whole lot of oil and flour in our jar. Maybe we only have a little. Maybe we have got a real big flour jar, or perhaps a very small one. No matter what we have, we can still learn to live with a generous spirit.

Here are some questions we might want to ask occasionally:

- Am I being faithful with my tithe to God?
- Am I being responsive to the needs of the poor?
- Am I learning to take risks in giving that stretch my faith?
- Am I giving in a way that is becoming a natural part of how I live?
- Am I noticing God's generous provision in my life and responding with a thankful heart?

Dallas Willard says the law of the kingdom is the law of inversion, where the last are first and the servants are the greatest. This is modeled in a striking way in the life of this widow. The weakest, most vulnerable person—an impoverished, pagan, Gentile widow—becomes the one whose generosity keeps the prophet Elijah alive. What an amazing example for all of us!

If you were the widow in this story, how do you think you would have responded to Elijah's request?

2

What do you think the widow learned about God and herself through this experience?

Which person has modeled a surprisingly generous heart and lifestyle for you, and how has he or she impacted your life?

3

What is one step you can take in becoming a more generous person?

Give all He asks; Take all He gives.
THOMAS R. KELLY

Read: 1 Kings 18:16–39

WHERE IS BAAL TODAY?
Few people actually bow down and worship stone idols these days. But idolatry is still present in our day. Anything we allow to take the place of God in our lives can become a Baal. The things we try to embrace and cling to while we still hold onto God can become idolatrous.

A Baal is *anything* that tempts us away from full devotion to God. For example, a Baal can be:

- a *relationship* that dishonors God
- a *lifestyle* that keeps you from being generous to the poor
- a *habit* or an *addiction* that you know God wants you to give up but you refuse
- a *grudge* against someone who has hurt you
- a struggle with *pride* and the power it has over you

We are all tempted to tell ourselves that we can hang onto our idols and God at the same time. What God taught the people of Israel, and what he wants to teach us, is that it is impossible to hold both God and idols in our heart. There is simply not enough room.

4

Imagine you are one of the people in the crowd who is standing on Mount Carmel and is watching the battle between Elijah and the prophets of Baal. Years later, when you tell your grandchildren what happened on that mountain, what would you tell them about one of the following lessons:

- What did you learn about Yahweh, the God of Israel?
- What did you discover about Baal and idol worship?
- How did you see God at work in Elijah?
- What did you learn about yourself?

5

If we understand idolatry to be anything that keeps us from loving God fully, what is one place that idolatry has crept into your life?

What is one step you can take to get rid of it?

Read: 1 Kings 19:1–9

FROM THE MOUNTAIN TO THE VALLEY

How many people in the history of the human race have ever experienced manifestations of God's power as Elijah did? He saw God work in ways most of us could never even dream possible. Yet, right after seeing God pour fire from heaven and defeat the prophets of Baal, things take a dramatic turn for Elijah.

When Jezebel hears of Elijah's triumph over her prophets, she vows to see him dead. Elijah, who has defied a king, defeated 850 prophets, and confronted an entire nation single-handedly, is running in fear at the threat of one queen. This turnabout is so sudden and so dramatic that some Old Testament scholars are convinced this part of the story is out of place. However, there is nothing in the text or in life to support this idea.

Elijah experiences what many followers of Christ have gone through. After a mountaintop experience of intense intimacy with God and awareness of God's presence, Elijah hits a low point in his spiritual life. He goes from the mountain to the valley.

Some say that there is no way that the bold, confrontational, and fearless Elijah we meet in 1 Kings 18 is the same man we find in this passage. As you look at both of these passages, how do you explain the radically different responses we see in Elijah?

6

7 Tell about a time you experienced a spiritual high point in your life and then faced the reality of a spiritual low point.

How was God with you both on the heights of the mountaintop and the depths of the valley?

Read: 1 Kings 19:10–18

A FRESH START

God sees Elijah in the midst of his time of turmoil and God cares. He does an amazing thing. As Elijah pours out his heart, God begins a process of giving him a whole new beginning. He calls him out of the cave and into the light. On the mountain Elijah stands and waits for the Lord to pass by. First, there is a powerful wind, then there is an earthquake, and finally a fire. But God is not in these things. Finally, there is a gentle whisper and God is there, with Elijah, showing him that he still sees and cares.

At this time, God lets Elijah know that he can have a fresh start. He reminds him that he is not alone and that there are many who still follow Yahweh. And, best of all, God begins to reveal his plan to bring a new friend into Elijah's life, a man named Elisha, who will follow in his steps as a prophet. God is not even close to being done with working in Elijah's life.

E xtraordinary afflictions are not always the punishment of extraordinary sins, but sometimes the trial of extraordinary graces. Sanctified afflictions are spiritual promotions.

MATTHEW HENRY

What did God say and do that brings hope to Elijah at this pivotal time in his life?

8

God let Elijah know that he still has ministry to do, new mountains to climb, and lives to impact. Why is having a clear purpose in life so important if we are going to move forward with hope and confidence?

9

Tell about a time when God gave you a new vision and a fresh beginning in some area of your life. How has your life changed since that time of new beginnings?

10

Closing Reflection

Take a few minutes of silence for personal reflection . . .

Is there an area of your life where you need a new beginning today? How can your small group pray for you as you seek God's power to take new steps for God in this area of your life?

Take time to respond to this closing question:

> *What can your small group members do to help you as you get started in this area of your life?*

Close your small group by praying together . . .

- Pray for each member of your small group to experience a fresh beginning in one area of life.

- Ask the Holy Spirit to lead them and sustain them as they offer this area over to him.

Old Testament Life Challenge

HOW DO WE PRAY?

It is helpful to observe the vivid contrast between the way the prophets of Baal pray and the way Elijah prays. The 850 false prophets yell, scream, act out, and put on a show. Elijah simply speaks and watches God manifest his power.

This is important to note because sometimes Christians pray more like the prophets of Baal than like Elijah. They pray as if they think that they have to get God's attention by doing something dramatic. Some followers of Christ believe they must pray loud enough, long enough, with the right formula, with enough boldness, or with some kind of radical and special behavior if God is going to hear. This is simply not true. Elijah talks to God calmly and expects God to take care of the results.

Pay attention to your prayers in the coming days. Do you pray with the calm assurance of Elijah or the ravings of the prophets of Baal? Learn to come before God, knowing that he hears your prayers when you lift them to him in Jesus' name. He hears, not because you speak loud enough or because you repeat the same words over and over again; rather, he hears because you are his child and you bring your prayers to him in the name of Jesus Christ.

Elisha: Receiving a Spiritual Legacy

SESSION 2: 1 KINGS 19:15–21; 2 KINGS 2:1–15; 4:1–7; 6:8–23

Introduction

In ancient Greece when it was time for the Olympic Games, athletes from around the country were handed a torch with a special flame. Every one ran his leg of the race and then handed off the torch to the next runner. Eventually the torch made it to an altar in Olympia and remained there. Other flames came and went, but this one was never to be extinguished.

This was a sacred matter to the Greek people. The flame symbolized the light of spirit and knowledge and life that gets passed down from one generation to another. These people considered themselves keepers of the flame. They were passers of the torch.

At the beginning of time, God lit a flame and passed it on. It started with Adam and Eve. Later, Abraham passed the torch to Isaac, who in turn handed it to Jacob and thence to Joseph. In the Bible, passing the flame did not just happen between parents and children. Moses passed the torch to Joshua. Eli did the same with young Samuel. Jesus passed the torch to his apostles. The apostle Paul, as an old man, celebrated as he saw the flame of faith ignite in Timothy's life.

From the beginning, God planned for his followers to be torchbearers. If we fail to rise up to this calling, each new generation is at risk! The question God is asking is clear: "Will somebody guard the flame? Will we continue the legacy and pass on the torch to the next generation?"

Looking at Life

Who was a spiritual torch-passer in your life, and how has that person's life impacted yours?

1

Who is one person (or group of people) whom God has called you to influence, and how are you passing on the torch of faith?

Learning from the Word
Read: 1 Kings 19:15–21

MAKING SACRIFICES

What Elijah is asking Elisha to do in this story involves enormous sacrifice. The Bible says nothing about Elijah's background. He may well have been from a poor family. He may not have had too many career options. But Elisha is another story. This passage makes it clear that Elisha comes from a very wealthy family (they have twelve yoke of oxen). Elisha has it made. He will inherit a way of life that will keep him comfortable for the rest of his days.

But God has called Elijah to ask Elisha to walk away from his secure and wealthy lifestyle and follow him on a path that may easily lead to poverty, rejection, and the opposition of stubborn kings who want him dead. From the beginning, Elisha must have realized that following God's plan for his life means making significant sacrifices.

2

When Elijah invites Elisha to become a prophet and follow in his footsteps, he calls Elisha to take a bold and sacrificial step of faith. How might some of the following people have responded to Elijah's bold invitation?

- Elisha's parents
- Elisha
- the people living in Elisha's hometown

How does Elijah exercise faith by making the request of Elisha?

Tell about a time when God called you to make a sacrifice so that you could live more fully for him. How has your response to God's invitation impacted your life?

Tell about a time that you made what felt like a sacrifice for God, but later you realized that you gained more than you sacrificed.

> Never insult anybody
> by asking them to do an easy job.
>
> **MAX DEPREE**

Read: 2 Kings 2:1–15

THE FLAME IS PASSED

Before Elijah is taken from Elisha, Elijah asks what he can do for him. Elisha requests an inheritance of a double portion of Elijah's spirit. Elisha asks for exactly the right thing. Elijah lets him know that what he has asked for is difficult, though not impossible. When it comes to choosing his successor, in the final view, no mere human being can do that. Elijah can help, shape, and encourage, but ultimately Elisha's work is between him and God.

Elijah says, "If you see me when I'm taken from you, it will be yours." Tension is now introduced to the story. Not only is Elisha going to lose Elijah, he doesn't know if his own ministry is just beginning or about to end. As they wait to see what God is going to do, they walk together. This is a beautiful picture of two friends walking along the Jordan side by side. We can only imagine what is going through their minds. They have traveled so many miles together. God has used them to do amazing things. They have forged a friendship. But soon, Elisha will be alone. What will his future look like?

Suddenly, out of nowhere, a chariot of fire and horses of fire appear, and the two men are separated from each other. Elijah is swept up into the arms of God, and Elisha is left behind. Elisha cries out, "My father! My father!" He sees the whole thing. His friend, mentor, and leader is gone, so he tears his garments—a sign of grief and loss.

Elisha looks down on the ground and sees Elijah's cloak. It's his reminder of the torch that has been passed to him. He picks up the mantle and walks back and stands on the bank of the Jordan. What a pivotal moment in Elisha's life. He takes the cloak and rolls it up, just as he had seen Elijah do. He lifts his arm, just as he had seen Elijah do. And he swallows hard, gets ready, and strikes the water of the Jordan.

The water parts, and Elisha crosses on dry ground. The mantle has been passed, the Spirit is alive in Elisha, and he is ready to be a torchbearer for God.

4

Why do you think Elijah keeps saying, "Stay here"? And why do you think Elisha keeps saying, "As surely as the LORD lives and you live, I will not leave you"?

What do you think is going through Elisha's mind as he stands at the bank of the Jordan with Elijah's mantle in his hand?

5

What can we do to thank, affirm, and bless the torchbearers who have impacted our lives?

What are some of the practical steps we can take to have a torch-bearing impact on others?

Read: 2 Kings 4:1–7

A BIG-JAR GOD!

God gives this widow, her sons, all Israel, and all who read the Bible an unforgettable lesson: "Don't ask for just a few. If you give God a few jars; he'll fill a few. If we give him a lot of jars, he'll fill a lot." In this story we learn that our God is a big-jar God! He has the resources to fill every jar we bring to him.

God comes to us today and asks, "What do you have?" We may look and say, "Nothing!" But God says, "Look closer." If all we have is a little oil, God can multiply it and provide all we need. The same God who gave manna in the desert, who delivered meals special delivery by ravens, who sent angels to bring cakes in the desert, can fill our jars also. We need to look at the little we have and place it in the hands of our big-jar God and watch what he can do with it!

What steps of faith do the widow and her sons have to take before they will see the miraculous provision of God?

6

Tell about a time God called you to take a step of faith that preceded his provision in your life.

When Elisha asks the woman, "What do you have in your house?" she answered, "A little oil." Today God asks you: What do you have in your house? What can you give to him or use for his glory? What do you have that you can offer to God today?

7

Read: 2 Kings 6:8-23

OPEN MY EYES!

Many followers of Christ need to hear the words: "Don't be afraid. Those who are with us are more than those who are with them." Whatever we face—problems, challenges, difficulties, fears, or worries—we all have times we need to have our eyes shifted from earthly to heavenly realities. Sometimes we need to ask God to show us what is happening in the heavenly realms so that we can walk with courage in this life.

At other times, we must pray for faith to believe what our eyes cannot see. Like the servant of Elisha, we need to learn that those who are with us, when we stand with the Lord, are always more than those who are with them.

8 What do each of the following people learn about God's power and character?

- Elisha's servant
- the soldiers in the Aramean army
- the king of Aram
- the king of Israel

9 What is one situation in your life in which you need to have your eyes opened to see God's presence and power revealed?

10 How can your small group members pray for you and support you as you wait to see God's glory revealed in this area of your life?

Closing Reflection

Take a few minutes of silence for personal reflection . . .

Think about those who have passed on the torch of faith to you. Think also of those to whom you have passed on the flame. Thank God for the torch-bearing ministry that is given to every follower of Christ.

Take time to respond to this closing question:

> *What would happen in your church if all those who follow Jesus failed to fulfill the call to be part of God's torch-passing ministry?*

Close your small group by praying together . . .

- Take time to pray for God to move followers of Christ in two different directions. First, ask for a sense of praise and thankfulness to overflow for those who have passed on the torch of faith to us. Celebrate how God has used family members, friends, neighbors, Sunday school teachers, youth leaders, pastors, and others to pass on the flame. Second, ask for the power of the Holy Spirit to fill each Christ-follower with the strength and boldness he or she needs to be a bearer of the torch and a keeper of the flame. Ask God to help us pass the flame to a new generation.

Old Testament Life Challenge

LOOKING BACK AND LOOKING FORWARD

Every follower of Christ is where he or she is because somebody passed on the torch of faith. Maybe it was parents, grandparents, a teacher, a Sunday school teacher, a school teacher, a pastor, or someone else, but somebody nurtured our faith. Someone prayed, invested, loved, and let the flame of faith burn bright. It is important we all understand that in every generation, from Abraham's to ours, somebody passed the torch to somebody else and then to somebody else. Not a single generation has been skipped. That is why we are where we are today.

Take a moment to reflect on these questions:

- Whom did God use to pass on the flame of faith to me?

- Who has prayed for me, loved me, and let their light shine for me?

- Who has been a torchbearer in my life?

- How can I thank or bless those who have been used to pass on the torch in my life?

Next, take a moment to reflect on these questions:

- Do I have people in my life to whom I am passing the torch?

- In whom am I investing myself?

- Am I keeping the flame bright in my life so that the torch gets passed on to others?

- Who are specific people whom God has placed in my life so that I can pass the flame to them?

- What are some of the steps I can take to more intentionally be a torchbearer in the lives of others?

Amos: How to Measure a Life

SESSION 3: AMOS 2:6–4:3; 5:21–24; DEUTERONOMY 24:12–13, 17–22

Introduction

The Bible is filled with examples of people who spoke words of amazing boldness. Here are just a few examples:

When David faced Goliath and this human tank threatened to give his flesh to the birds and animals of the field (and he meant this literally), this was David's response:

> "You come against me with sword and spear and javelin, but I come against you in the name of the LORD Almighty, the God of the armies of Israel, whom you have defied. This day the LORD will hand you over to me, and I'll strike you down and cut off your head. Today I will give the carcasses of the Philistine army to the birds of the air and the beasts of the earth, and the whole world will know that there is a God in Israel." (1 Samuel 17:45–46)

When John the Baptist met the religious leaders of his day, this was his greeting:

> "You brood of vipers! Who warned you to flee from the coming wrath? Produce fruit in keeping with repentance. And do not think you can say to yourselves, 'We have Abraham as our father.' I tell you that out of these stones God can raise up children for Abraham. The ax is already at the root of the trees, and every tree that does not produce good fruit will be cut down and thrown into the fire." (Matthew 3:7–10)

When the apostle Paul stood before King Agrippa and boldly presented the gospel, Agrippa asked this question: "Do you think that in such a short time you can persuade me to be a Christian?" Paul's response is heartfelt and incredibly bold:

> "Short time or long—I pray God that not only you but all who are listening to me today may become what I am, except for these chains." (Acts 26:29)

All sorts of people in the Bible spoke with great clarity and boldness.

Looking at Life

1 What is one bold statement you have made that took more courage than you knew you had?

What was it that moved you to a place of speaking with this level of boldness?

Learning from the Word
Read: Amos 2:6–16 and Deuteronomy 24:12–13, 17–22

THE HEART OF GOD

In this passage of Amos, God does not say that the people of Israel don't worship enough. He doesn't say that they don't know the Scriptures. He doesn't say a whole lot of things we might have expected him to say. He says, "My heart is broken over the way my people hoard their resources and neglect the poor while they claim to follow and know me."

God is deeply concerned about our worship. He cares very much that we know the teaching of Scripture. God wants us to attend church services and share in life-giving fellowship among his people. But this is not the whole story! When we truly worship God, our hearts are captured by the things that matter to God—and God cares about the poor, the oppressed, and the outcast. When we study the Bible, we should follow what it teaches. This means we should learn from Amos and begin to act in ways that will bring justice for those who are marginalized. God longs to see a balance in the lives of his followers. Spirit-led worship should lead to passionate service and compassionate acts of justice.

Here are two more passages that communicate the heart of God:

> He who is kind to the poor lends to the LORD,
> and he will reward him for what he has done. (Proverbs 19:17)

> A father to the fatherless, a defender of widows,
> is God in his holy dwelling. (Psalm 68:5)

All through the Old Testament God expresses his heart toward the marginalized, and he invites us to join in his commitment to bring love and justice to those who often don't receive it.

When the police have witnesses give testimony about what they have seen at a crime scene, they begin to draw a composite, a picture, of the suspect they are trying to apprehend. Imagine that those writing or speaking in the five passages listed above (Deuteronomy 24:12–13; 24:17–22; Amos 2:6–16; Proverbs 19:17; Psalm 68:5) are giving testimony about the character of God. If you were drawing a composite sketch, what kind of insight do you get about the heart of God? What does he love and what does he hate?

2

Amos is specific about the sins being committed by the people of Israel. What are these sins and how are these same sins alive and active in the world today?

3

What are some of the injustices that can slip into our lives when we are not being careful and sensitive to the heart of God?

4

Ｗe choose to be poor for the love of God. In the service of the poorest of the poor, we are feeding the hungry Christ, clothing the naked Christ, and giving shelter to the homeless Christ.

MOTHER TERESA OF CALCUTTA

Read: Amos 2:6 and 3:15–4:3

THE FEET OF MOTHER TERESA AND THE APPETITES OF THE ISRAELITE WOMEN

Here are two short stories of radically different women.

A story is told of a man who spent time serving with Mother Teresa in Calcutta. Once, while working at her side, he noticed that her feet were badly misshapen. This troubled him. But, he did not ask her about it. Later on, he asked somebody in the community about her feet.

He was told that among the poor there are never enough shoes. Mother Teresa always insisted that when shoes were donated, the best pairs always be given away to the most poor. She always took the worst for herself—whatever was left over. As the years passed, her feet became badly deformed. For Mother Teresa, consistent acts of compassion for the poor cost her something. Compassion always does.

In the days of Amos the wealthy women had become both fat and addicted to wine. Amos actually called them "cows of Bashan." Bashan was a fertile area where the cows were famous for being well fed and large! This is not just random name-calling. Cows are a walking appetite. They actually have four stomachs and they are eating machines. They consume—it's what they do best! The only question they ask is, "Where can I get more?"

5

Amos shares God's concern for justice. He is concerned that the people of his day have fallen into the "cows of Bashan syndrome." Simply put, this is when a person wants more and more. Then, when they get it, they want even more! How do you see the "cows of Bashan syndrome" at work in our world today?

6

What does the "cows of Bashan syndrome" look like when it creeps into the church and into the lives of followers of Christ?

What are practical steps we can take to combat this syndrome and drive it out of our lives and churches?

7

Read: Amos 5:21-24

A CALL TO JUSTICE

In one of the great statements in all the Bible Amos unveils the heart of God: "But let justice roll on like a river, righteousness like a never-failing stream!" (Amos 5:24). God is saying, "Let justice and compassion flow out of your lives. Don't sit there eating vast amounts of food at your religious feasts while the poor are starving to death outside your door and while you congratulate yourselves on how much you love me. It is time for the earth to be covered with rivers of righteousness and justice, and my people are the ones I will use to make this dream a reality."

As followers of Jesus we need to identify the ways God can use us to let justice and righteousness flow across this earth. Local churches need to be places where the marginalized know they are welcomed and loved. We even need to go a step further and find those who are outcast and extend to them the loving mercy of God.

God wants our heart to beat with his heart. What can we do to grow a heart that longs for justice and righteousness to flow?

8

What is one act of justice you can begin to live out in your personal life? How can your small group members encourage you as you seek to grow in this area of justice?

9

10 What justice-filled action can your small group take that will bring a measure of God's righteousness in your community?

Closing Reflection

Take a few minutes of silence for personal reflection . . .

Invite the Holy Spirit to gently begin to show you where the "cows of Bashan syndrome" has crept into your life.

Take time to respond to this closing question:

How can you grow in righteousness and justice and resist the temptation to live like a cow of Bashan?

Close your small group by praying together . . .

- Pray for those (yourself included, if this is appropriate) who have been swept up into the "cows of Bashan" frenzy of our culture. Ask God to help each person see a new vision of what life can really mean.

- Pray for those who are seeking to do justice and let righteousness flow like a river. Ask God to bring them joy and strength to continue moving forward.

- Finally, pray for the local church to grow in a commitment to accomplish God's justice in a world that so desperately needs to see God's love modeled in our actions.

Old Testament Life Challenge

HOW DO WE MEASURE OUR LIVES?

In our world, we like to measure ourselves by comparing ourselves to others. We don't like unchanging standards. We can always find somebody who is worse than us, greedier than us, and further away from God's standards than us. It's tempting to try to evade God's Word and standards by comparing ourselves to other people or to society as a whole. We can do this in many areas of life:

- *Generosity:* We can say, "My heart's generous. I want to be generous. I just don't have very much money right now. Things are kind of tight. Someday, I'll have more money and then I'll help take care of people who are in need." But for now, we go on spending every dime we have on ourselves.
- *Serving:* We can say, "I'm really busy right now. I'd love to serve people who are in need, but I can't fit it into my schedule. Maybe when I have more time and get on top of things, then I will serve those in need." But, our schedule never seems to open up and serving never fits into our day planner.
- *Reaching out:* We can say, "I'd love to form a relationship with somebody of a different ethnicity or in a different culture. I really want to be part of God's solution to breaking down the walls that divide us, but it involves taking risks, and I am not up for that. I will wait for someone else to reach out to me; then maybe I can respond instead of initiate." But time passes and the walls grow higher and higher.

We can measure our lives by comparing ourselves with others, but God does not. He sets a standard that is radically different from the constantly changing world in which we live. We need to look to his Word and discover his standard and then ask him for the strength to grow in our devotion to live with the justice, righteousness, and compassion that marks the heart of God.

God says, "I will measure my people by the one standard that counts. And it's a real simple standard. Are there hungry people? Feed them. Are there sick people? Help them. Are there oppressed people? Stick up for them. Are there lonely widows? Visit them. Are there uneducated children? Teach them. Are there people who get rejected because of the color of their skin? Befriend them."

Isaiah: Pursuing Spiritual Authenticity

SESSION 4: ISAIAH 6:1-9a; 49:6; 2 CHRONICLES 26:1-15; EXODUS 3:5;
LEVITICUS 11:44-45; 1 PETER 1:13-16

Introduction

Channel surfing is the exercise of sitting riveted to a television set and
going from channel to channel, often at a fairly rapid pace. Some people
can spend a whole evening, a Saturday, or even an entire weekend surfing
from channel to channel.

We have all spent some time channel surfing. What we discover, with
time, is that it never changes our lives for the better. We will never hear
someone say, "Last night I channel surfed all night long, from dinner until
midnight, and I'm so glad I did. It was such a great experience. I feel like a
new person today."

The truth of the matter is that most time spent channel surfing ends
up being wasted time. It is the time we unplug our brains, put everything
in neutral, and "veg out."

Surprisingly, there are people who take the time to study things like
channel surfing. Their studies tell us that habitual channel surfing can
have negative effects of us. It decreases our attention span and increases
our sense of isolation and passivity. The obvious question is, if channel
surfing takes away so many hours of our life and gives so little back, why
do we do it?

Looking at Life

If channel surfing takes so much from us and gives so little back, why do
we do it? What explanation can you give for the highly popular
phenomenon of channel surfing?

1

Learning from the Word
Read: Isaiah 6:1–8; 2 Chronicles 26:1–15

THE YEAR UZZIAH DIED

Isaiah 6 begins with the words: "In the year that King Uzziah died." Isaiah starts with these words for specific reasons. Uzziah became king of Israel when he was only sixteen years old. He was a remarkable leader (see the list of his accomplishments in 2 Chronicles 26). He was a military genius. He built an army of more than 300,000 soldiers. He built machines designed by skillful men that could shoot arrows and sling large rocks. Under him, the Philistines were finally defeated. Other enemies, like the Ammonites, brought tribute to him.

He was also a builder. He fortified the walls of Jerusalem so that city was finally safe. He was a technological innovator and an economic wizard. He developed a widespread system of cisterns for gathering water and developed Israel's agricultural economy.

Uzziah was also a spiritual leader. He was instructed and trained to follow God by a prophet named Zechariah, so that he did what was right in the eyes of the Lord. His fame spread as far as Egypt. With the possible exception of Solomon, he was one of the most powerful kings the southern kingdom of Judah ever had.

2

From what you learn in these passages about King Uzziah, why was Isaiah's vision so important and timely for the people of God?

3

What are some times in our lives during which we easily forget that God is on the throne? What can we do to turn our eyes toward heaven and grow in our recognition that God is reigning in power, even when our life experiences do not fully bear out this truth?

Read: Isaiah 6:2–3; Exodus 3:5; Leviticus 11:44–45; 1 Peter 1:13–16

HEAVENLY BEINGS

As Isaiah sees the glory of the King of heaven, he also sees that God is surrounded by angelic beings. Isaiah tries to communicate this spiritual reality. He points out that the seraphs used two wings to cover their faces. They are covering their faces because of the unspeakable holiness of God. We are told that no one can see God's face and live, and these beings get the point. They are not fallen, but even they do not dare look directly on the glory of God.

These heavenly beings are covering their feet with another set of wings. Back in those days, feet were a sign of earthliness. They were the body part that connected people to the ground, so covering them was a sign of honor and respect. Note Exodus 3:5, for when God revealed himself to Moses through the burning bush, he said, "Take off your sandals, for the place where you are standing is holy ground."

Then, amid the smoke and earthquake-like atmosphere, we hear the heavenly beings cry out, "Holy, holy, holy is the LORD Almighty; the whole earth is full of his glory" (Isaiah 6:3). This threefold affirmation of God's holiness was the Hebrew way of giving emphasis. In the Bible there are other words and attributes of God that are mentioned with a double affirmation. Only God's holiness is repeated three times in a row!

In light of what Isaiah and Moses experienced, give a definition of what the Bible means when it says that God is holy.

4

How should the holiness of God impact the way we approach him and relate to him?

5

How should the holiness of God impact the way we live?

Read: Isaiah 6:5–7

"A LITTLE CREASE"

Faced with God's holiness, Isaiah sees himself as he is. In response, he speaks the truth about his own condition. This is rare! More often, we look at ourselves and downplay our sin and weaknesses. We suffer from something called a self-serving bias. That is, we minimize the reality of our sin, the cost of our wrong choices, and the damage we have done to others and ourselves.

Imagine a teenage son who borrows his father's car for the first time. He has permission, and his father gives detailed instructions on the use of this particular automobile. While pulling into a parking space, the teenage son hits the side of the car on a light post. When he gets out of the car and looks at the damage, he sees a long scrape in the paint and a crease in the body of the car. He calls his father and tries to explain what happened.

"I was being very careful. I didn't see the light post there. It's really just a little scrape and a small crease in the body of the car. I don't think it will cost much to fix it." When the teenage son gives this information, he really means it. He hopes it is no big deal. His own self-serving bias leads him to believe it is not a big problem and that someone can probably pound the crease out with relative ease.

The next day, in broad daylight, the man at the body shop has a whole different understanding of the extent of the damage. He sees things the way they really are. He knows the real damage, and he knows the cost involved in repairing this "little crease."

6

How does a self-serving bias affect the way we view our own sin?

What are some examples of how we can downplay the impact of our sin and rationalize continuing on a sinful path?

What is one area of life in which you need to set aside a self-serving bias and really see sin for what it is?

7

How can your small group members pray for you and keep you accountable to walk in holiness in this area of your life?

> *L*ike the face of the mythical Medusa, our true condition, away from God, would turn us to stone if we ever fully confronted it. It would drive us mad. But if we saw ourselves in the light of God's holiness, we literally could not survive it. Emotionally, psychologically, we literally could not survive it.
>
> **DALLAS WILLARD**

Read: Isaiah 6:8–9a and 49:6

MOVING INTO ACTION

God doesn't cleanse Isaiah just for his own sake. God has a calling for him. God says, "Whom shall I send? And who will go for us?" Of course, God is not perplexed about this. He asks the question so that Isaiah can freely choose to go.

Isaiah says, "Here am I. Send me!" Spiritually authentic worship always ends with a heart that is willing to follow God. Worship is never just about having an intense emotional experience. It is never simply about how I feel when I am finished. Authentic worship always costs something. It costs us a submitted life.

For Isaiah, and for us, authentic time in the presence of God will give us a passion to reach out to people who still need to meet God in all of his holiness. As we experience the cathartic cleansing that comes when a repentant heart meets God's searing holiness, we long for others to have this same life-changing experience. True worship propels us out with the message that God loves his children and is ready to cleanse us and give us a new beginning!

8 Isaiah has a life-changing vision of God. He comes to a place of brokenness and repentance. Then God calls him out to do his work and to bring the message of the light that is for all the nations of the world. Why is this process of seeing God, repenting, and moving into ministry so important for Isaiah and for us?

9 Which of these three things needs to happen more in your life right now?

- a clearer vision of God
- a deeper level of repentance in your heart
- a greater commitment to do ministry that spreads God's light

What step can you take to grow in your vision, repentance, or commitment to ministry?

Closing Reflection

Take a few minutes of silence for personal reflection . . .

Isaiah is clear that God's grace, power, and love are not just for the people of Israel, but they are for all people (Isaiah 49:6). Think about the people in your life, neighborhood, workplace, and social circles who do not have a relationship with God through Jesus Christ. Reflect on ways God might use you to let his light shine into their lives.

Take time to respond to this closing question:

What one person in your life needs to see God's holiness, repent of his or her sin, and experience a new beginning because of God's grace?

Close your small group by praying together . . .

- Ask God to help you consistently pray for this person.

- Seek God's wisdom and direction on how you might be used to show his love to this person.

Old Testament Life Challenge

SETTING ASIDE DISTRACTIONS

True worship is always costly. It is the opposite of casual. It involves an investment of self. When we understand the nature of worship, we no longer make casual commitments. We don't say "if I have time," "if it's convenient," "if I like the style," or "when I can get around to it." We don't worship God with a casual spirit. We don't drift in and out of attention as we do when we are channel surfing.

As we grow in worship, we no longer have an attitude that says, "If something tickles my fancy, then I'll pay attention." We don't worship with a casual attitude. We can't stomach the idea of singing songs about devotion and then go and live the same old self-centered way.

True worship means that we learn to do what the angels did. We come with our whole person before God. We focus our thoughts and our emotions on him. We sing with all our heart, even when we don't really like the tune, because God deserves our undivided praise. We listen intently to the preached word even if the teaching style is not what we like, because we know that God wants to speak each time his Word is opened.

We set aside everything that could distract us, and we strain, with all our strength, to see the Lord seated on his throne. We do all we can to enter the presence of God, who is high and exalted. We stand in awe of his majestic glory, and we respond to him with our voices, bodies, hearts, lives, and all that is in us. When we commit to worship, we decide to take every possible distraction and set it aside because we are going to worship the God who made us and loves us.

For the next few weeks, pay attention to how you worship.

- What tends to distract you?

- How can you learn to live with these distractions or get rid of them?

- Are you taking time to get good rest so you are fresh and awake when you come to worship?

- Are you giving 100 percent of yourself when you worship?

Hezekiah: Radical Trust

Introduction

These passages record the stories of two radically different kings of Judah. Ahaz is an example of a life driven by fear. Rather than placing his trust in God, he trusts in military might and political alliances. In contrast, King Hezekiah stands as an example of radical trust in God. Rather than take the easy route of establishing strategic military and political alliances, he looks to God as his source of strength.

God invites us into a relationship based on trust. Though we live in a world that can cause great fear and anxiety, God offers another path. Radical trust is God's plan for all followers of Jesus. Through the example of Ahaz, we learn of the folly of fear, and through the life of Hezekiah, the pathway of trust.

Many devoted followers of Jesus face ongoing battles with fear and anxiety. They may ask the question, "Is it really possible to be free of fear? Can we live with a deep level of trust in God?" The apostle Paul gives this exhortation:

> *Do not be anxious about anything, but in everything, by prayer and petition, with thanksgiving, present your requests to God. And the peace of God, which transcends all understanding, will guard your hearts and your minds in Christ Jesus. (Philippians 4:6–7)*

Looking at Life

What are some of the things in our world that cause people to live with anxiety and fear?

1

Learning from the Word
Read: Isaiah 7:1–17

KEEPING YOUR OPTIONS OPEN

We might think that King Ahaz would be thrilled with the offer of a sign from God. Wouldn't he love some kind of sign to buttress his faith and guarantee that the nation of Judah would be safe? But his response is surprising and strange: "I will not ask; I will not put the LORD to the test" (Isaiah 7:12).

At first glance it seems as if Ahaz is being reverent by refusing a sign. He appears to be doing the honorable thing. But this is not the case. Ahaz is covering his real intentions with a thin veneer of piety and spirituality. The reason Ahaz won't ask God for a sign is that he wants to keep his options open. He wants to be able to jump in and follow God, or go the other way and disobey God if that seems like the better option.

Ahaz knows if he asks for a sign, God will give it and then his options will be limited. If he enters a conversation with God and agrees to submit to God, he will slam the door on the Assyrian option. Ahaz wants to keep his options open more than he wants to obey God.

It's scary to say, "I'm going to cut myself off from my sinful options. I'm only going to speak truth. I'm not going to spin or manipulate anyone." This intentional limiting of options will be new territory for many people. Too many followers of Christ do exactly as Ahaz does here. Because of fear and anxiety, we leave our options open and dishonor God in the process.

Isaiah goes to incredible lengths to help Ahaz turn from fear and to learn how to trust in God. Ahaz has every opportunity to limit his options and surrender to God's will. In the same way, God invites us to willingly limit our options. Taking this step can look different for each person who is seeking to be fully devoted to God.

2

God offers to give Ahaz a sign, but he refuses it. But God gives him a sign anyway. What sign does God promise Ahaz, and how does this prophetic sign still bring freedom from fear today?

Ahaz has a fear problem. Rather than trusting God, he looks to his own wisdom and the military might of other nations to deliver him. In what areas of our lives might we be tempted to place our trust?

3

Why is placing trust in these things always a mistake?

What is one biblical or spiritual lesson you have learned that helps you keep from being consumed by fear?

4

If our lives are driven by fear, what are some of the possible consequences?

Read: Isaiah 36:1–37:20

A NEW TIME AND A NEW KING

In Isaiah 36 we meet a new king of Judah and discover another way to live. This story takes place several decades after Ahaz was king of Judah. The northern kingdom—Israel—no longer exists. Although Assyria swallowed it up in 712 B.C., one thing has remained the same. There is political turmoil and the same superpower, Assyria, is threatening to conquer Judah.

The nation of Judah is standing strong, and much of their resolve comes from the courage of their king, Hezekiah. The current king of Assyria, Sennacherib, is prepared to squash Judah like a bug. But he prefers to have Judah surrender so he won't have to lose any soldiers. The time of Hezekiah is much like that of Ahaz, but he responds in a radically different way.

What do you do when you get a letter from the most powerful and bloodthirsty ruler in the world to inform you that he will be dropping in for a personal visit? How do you respond when you get the worst news of your life? Where do you turn when fear comes pounding on your front door?

The example of Hezekiah at this moment stands as a beacon for all who want to learn how to follow God. Hezekiah goes to the one place where answers are found, courage is gathered, and hope is restored. He goes to prayer—the throne of God!

5 What are some of the situations King Hezekiah faces that could cause him to be paralyzed by fear?

6 Rather than be ruled by fear, Hezekiah turns to God in prayer (Isaiah 37:14–20). What aspects of King Hezekiah's prayer can become an example of how we can pray when fear and anxiety come knocking on our door?

7 Describe a time when you faced a fear-producing situation and you turned to God in prayer. How did God answer and help you through this time?

P rayer is the key that unlocks all the storehouses of God's infinite grace and power. All that God is, and all that God has, is at the disposal of prayer.

R. A. TORREY

Read: Isaiah 37:21–38

ON THE LIGHTER SIDE: BAMBI VERSUS GODZILLA
Back in the late 1960s a short film named "Bambi Meets Godzilla" came out. It was a very, very, very short movie. It opened with some credits. Then there was a little deer grazing in a field (animated). As serene, quiet music played, a giant foot came down from above and squashed Bambi. Then the credits rolled. That was the end of the movie.

In the minds of both the Assyrians and the people of Judah, their battle will be a lot like "Bambi Meets Godzilla." Sennacherib, the king of Assyria, is absolutely certain that his military machine will run over Judah and hardly feel the speed bump as they do. Hezekiah faces the reality of this potential end to his kingship and nation, but he turns to God in prayer. What happens next gives hope to all who face tough odds but hold fast to God.

God gives a message to King Hezekiah through the prophet Isaiah (Isaiah 37:22–35). How is this prophetic message good news for Hezekiah and the nation of Judah, and how was it bad news for Sennacherib and the army of Assyria?

8

What is one fear you are facing in your life right now? What is one truth from this session you can apply to your situation today?

9

> Prayer is not overcoming Gods' reluctance; it is laying hold of His highest willingness.
>
> **RICHARD CHENEVIX TRENCH**

Closing Reflection

Take a few minutes of silence for personal reflection . . .

Identify one area where fear and anxiety have been setting into your life. What is the origin of this fear? How are you responding to this fear-producing situation? Are you bringing your fears and needs before God in prayer?

Take time to respond to this closing question:

> *How can your small group members pray for you and support you as you seek to trust in God and not let fear rule your life?*

Close your small group by praying together . . .

- Pray for each small group member who has shared about a potentially fear-producing situation they are facing. Pray for the peace of God's Spirit to fill them.

- Ask for courage to fill their heart. Call out to God to deliver them from this situation and reveal his glory and power.

Old Testament Life Challenge

WHAT DO YOU NEED TO BRING TO GOD?

Hezekiah takes the letter from Sennacherib and spreads it out before the Lord. He seeks the face of God in prayer, and God hears him. In response, Isaiah sends a message from God to Hezekiah. He assures him that his prayers have been heard and that the threats of Sennacherib will not come to pass.

Here is the question each person must ask: What do I need to spread out before the Lord?

Each of us gets letters from Assyria. A letter from Sennacherib can take many forms. It is anything that tempts us to be driven by fear. It is a piece of bad news that makes us so anxious that we feel paralyzed and unable to serve and live for God. It is a threat from a person that robs us of a sense of trust and confidence that God can deliver. It is anything that unleashes fear in our lives:

- Maybe it's a piece of paper from work that says your services are no longer required.

- Maybe it's an assignment that seems too hard, or a performance review that has you worried, or an expectation that you're not sure you can fulfill.

- Maybe it's a deep-rooted anxiety that rules your heart.

- Maybe it's a test at school.

- Maybe it's a looming black cloud of financial concerns.

- Maybe it's a word from a doctor or a diagnosis that's bad.

- Maybe it's a concern expressed by a teacher about one of your children.

- Maybe it's a word of rejection from someone you love.

- Maybe it's an email that cuts you deeply.

Hezekiah takes the worst letter with the worst news he's ever gotten in his life and spreads it out before the Lord. In response, God hears and answers. Like Hezekiah, we can bring our fear-producing, anxiety-building concerns before God in prayer. We can lay them down. We can place our trust in God rather than be ruled and driven by fear.

You may want to take a piece of paper and write down, clearly and specifically, what fear you are facing right now. Then, spread it before the Lord. Lay this paper before God and pray in utter honesty. Tell God your fears and ask for his deliverance!

Micah: Doing Justice

SESSION 6: ISAIAH 1:4–17; AMOS 4:1–6; MICAH 3:1–4; 2:11; 6:6–8

Introduction

We all look at the world through our own personal filters. If we feel happy and have our needs met, we tend to think the world is a pretty good place. When things are going well, we can often walk right past things that break the heart of God and not even notice them.

- We hear about violence on the news, but if it does not touch us or those close to us, it does not seem that important.
- We lie a little bit, but we comfort ourselves by thinking that this is common.
- We are unfaithful in thought or action, but we echo the old saying, "What my spouse doesn't know won't hurt him/her."
- We cheat in the workplace or school and justify it by saying that everyone does it.
- Eight thousand children and young people are infected with AIDS every single day in sub-Saharan Africa, but because it is so far away we hardly feel a thing.
- People in our country live on the streets and go to sleep with empty stomachs, and we learn to walk past them and look the other way. We convince ourselves that it is probably their own fault and they deserve the plight they are in.
- We get wrapped up in our own comfort, focus more and more on our wants, and quickly forget the needs of the poor and outcast.
- We get the paycheck we have worked so hard for and don't even think to give back to the God who has provided all that we have.

These things happen every day, every moment, and we say, "What's the big deal? That's life. It is just the way things are."

Looking at Life

1 What is an example of one specific injustice in our world and how people have become numb to it?

Learning from the Word
Read: Isaiah 1:4–17; Amos 4:1–6; Micah 3:1–4

HARSH PROPHETIC WORDS

The prophets call us to hear, see, and feel what we would miss on our own. It is easy for our hearts to become calloused and our eyes blinded to the sin in our lives, churches, and culture. The prophets strip away all of the facades and help us see ourselves as we really are.

The prophets call us to a deep level of self-examination and transformation. They remind us that God wants more than offerings and religious observance. He wants our hearts to beat in unison with his heart. He wants our lives to reflect the justice he wants to pour out on this earth. When we hear the voice of God speaking through the Old Testament prophets and when we respond to his call, we will see our lives, the church, and the world transformed.

2 In light of these three passages, what is the temperament of the prophets?

The prophet is a man who feels fiercely. God has thrust a burden upon his soul, and he is bowed and stunned at man's fierce greed. Prophecy is the voice God has lent to the silent agony. . . . God is raging in the prophet's words.

ABRAHAM HESCHEL

What do you learn about the heart and passion of God when you hear the voices of the prophets?

3

If we took the words of these prophets seriously, how might it impact *one* of the following areas of our lives?

4

- how we handle our financial resources
- how we worship God
- how we respond to the needs of the poor
- how we view "casual sin"

> **A**ll Scripture is God-breathed and is useful for teaching, rebuking, correcting and training in righteousness, so that the man of God may be thoroughly equipped for every good work.
>
> **THE APOSTLE PAUL (2 TIMOTHY 3:16–17)**

Read: Micah 2:11

OUR HEARTS HAVE BECOME NUMB

There are many things God wants us to see, but our eyes can be blind. There are truths the Holy Spirit is speaking to us, but we are often spiritually hard of hearing. Our hearts have become numb and we don't always get the subtle promptings of the Holy Spirit. The prophets speak with such conviction, clarity, and volume that they break through numb hearts. Micah uses the image of alcohol as he addresses the numb hearts of the people.

Just think about it for a minute. What is the effect of drinking beer or wine? Does it make a person more alert and sharp, or more comfortable and relaxed? The truth is, in general, drinking alcohol causes people to become mellow, relaxed, and less focused. Micah is making a powerful statement about the condition of the human heart. He says that people prefer to live in a state of spiritual inebriation. We don't want to notice, we prefer not to feel, we would rather not hear about all the pain in the world. If a prophet comes who brings words that made us feel comfortable, mellow, and relaxed, we love this prophet.

5

There are some false messages being proclaimed by modern-day "prophets," "teachers," and "preachers" that are designed to make people feel good. The problem is, these messengers are not telling the truth, or at least not the whole truth. What are some of these false messages?

6

Why is it essential for modern-day Christians to read the words of the prophets, even when they make us uncomfortable and shake us out of our spiritual inebriation?

7

Tell about a time when you were blinded and numb to an area of sin and God used the words of Scripture to splash ice-cold water in your face and wake you up to the truth.

The shallowness of our moral comprehension, the incapacity to sense the depth of misery caused by our own failures, is a simple fact of fallen humanity which no explanation can cover up.

ABRAHAM HESCHEL

Read: Micah 6:6-8

NOTICE THE ESCALATION

Micah asks a fundamental question: What can I bring to God? What does he really want from me? Then he begins to form a list of possible answers to this question. Notice how Micah begins small and then escalates.

- "Shall I come with *burnt offerings?*" Micah begins small. A burnt offering could be a dove or a pigeon—anyone could afford this.
- "Shall I come with *calves* a year old?" A calf was an expensive gift. Many families could not afford this kind of an offering; this would have been very generous.
- "Does God want *thousands of rams?*" This was an offering that only a king could give. The wealthiest person in all the land might be able to muster up this kind of an offering, but it is almost beyond imagination.
- "Would God like *ten thousand rivers of oil?*" This was simply impossible. Micah has now escalated the discussion to the point of being ridiculous. No person could offer God even one river of oil, much less ten thousand.
- "Should I offer *the life of my firstborn child?*" Micah knows that human sacrifice has been forbidden by God. He is not advocating human sacrifice in any way, shape, or form. He is simply escalating the discussion: Does God want me to give my child, that which is most precious to me in this world? Micah is pushing the discussion as far as he can.

After listing all kinds of offerings, Micah makes it clear that none of these is really what God wants. God is more concerned with the condition of our hearts and our daily lifestyle. In your own words, what are the three things God really wants from us?

8

9

In a practical, daily life way, what would it look like if you committed to do *one* of the following things:

- to act justly in your workplace and in your home
- to show mercy to those who live in your community and in your home
- to come before God with a genuinely humble heart

CAN I GIVE IT AWAY?

A mother and son were walking down a city street on a cold winter night. The little boy noticed a man huddled in an alley with only an old blanket to shelter him from the cold. He had never seen this sort of thing before. The mother was concerned for her son and began to pull him away from the situation. He resisted and asked if they could stop. The mother was anxious but willing to pause for just a moment. Her son motioned for her to lean over so he could say something. He whispered in her ear, "I have three more jackets at home, can I give that man my jacket?" His mother looked at him with surprise and concern. She paused and said. . .

10

What would you say if you were that mother?

How do you think this story should be finished?

> **I**f our goods are not available to the community, they are stolen goods.
>
> **MARTIN LUTHER**

Closing Reflection

Take a few minutes of silence for personal reflection . . .

Take time to reflect on where there might be injustice in specific areas of your life. Can you identify any injustice:

- in how you treat members of your family?

- in your local community?

- in your workplace?

- in your local church?

- in how you relate to your neighbors?

Take time to respond to these closing questions:

What is one step you need to take in an effort to live a life of justice where God has placed you?

Close your small group by praying together . . .
Pray in three specific directions:

- *Open our eyes:* Ask the Spirit to open eyes to see where sin has crept in and gone unnoticed.

- *Open our ears:* Ask God to sensitize the hearing of each person in your small group to receive what God wants to say through his prophets.

- *Soften our hearts:* Pray for hearts that are consistently tender and ready for transformation.

Old Testament Life Challenge

WHAT CAN ONE PERSON DO?

We can't correct all of the injustices in the world, but we can all do something. There are some first steps that will move a follower of Christ toward a deeper life of justice. Consider taking a step forward in one of the following ways:

- *Notice:* Ask God to help you tune in and notice injustice around you. This can be painful and cause discomfort, but it is critical for all who want to do justice. We must first learn to take note of where injustice exists. Part of this process is learning to notice where we are part of the injustice problem. When we see this, we must come before God and humbly seek his power to change.

• *Pray:* Every follower of Christ needs to learn the importance of praying for justice and against injustice. There is amazing power in prayer, and this is a critical starting point for Christ-followers.

• *Changed behavior:* God can help us learn to treat others fairly. Before we go seeking world justice, we need to be sure we are treating the people right around us with equity and justice. If God shows us an area in which we are being unjust in our treatment of another person, it is time to make some behavior and attitude adjustments.

• *Generosity:* If we have more than we need, we can begin to share with those who have needs. We can do it on our own, as we become aware of needs around us. We can also give through our church or other Christian organizations that provide for the basic needs of the poor.

Jeremiah: When God Gives a Hard Assignment

SESSION 7: JEREMIAH 1:4-10, 17-19; 20:1-2, 7-18; 37:15-16, 20

Introduction

Some people teach that following God leads to a safe, painless life. They tell us that if we are faithful to God's call, we will have protection from suffering and things will go our way. These folks have never encountered a prophet named Jeremiah.

Jeremiah lived with a heart that was humbly yielded to God. He heard the voice of the Father call him to proclaim the word of the Lord, and he lived with a tenacious obedience to this calling. But his faithfulness was met with resistance. His preaching was discarded and ignored. As he humbly followed God, he was mocked, rejected, beaten, imprisoned, and left to rot in a hole in the ground.

In the life of Jeremiah we learn that sometimes God calls his children to a hard assignment. Our responsibility is to follow, even through pain and tears. Through Jeremiah's example we discover that the life of faith can be like a marathon. We have to be ready to run hard, even when our bodies are weary and we feel like giving up.

Looking at Life

Tell about a time when God called you to do something that was hard. What did you learn from this experience?

1

Learning from the Word
Read: Jeremiah 1:4–10, 17–19

A STRONG START

In Jeremiah 1 we watch the prophet bolt from the starting blocks. He begins his race with passion and intensity. He's a young man, full of energy and optimism. He loves having a mission and a purpose for his life. Every indication is that Jeremiah leaves the gate running full speed!

We can almost hear him saying to himself, "I'm going to speak the words of God to whomever he tells me to speak them. No matter how much it costs me, I will fulfill my calling." Jeremiah is deeply committed to the call God has placed on his life. He is ready to run the race with all the strength he has.

Most followers of Christ can point back to some point in their spiritual life where they felt like Jeremiah at the start of his ministry. There was a time when God took hold of you and gave you a mission, a calling. It may have been during a camp experience as a young person. You felt God's call and said, "Wherever you lead, I will follow." Maybe it happened in a church service when the Holy Spirit spoke in power and you said, "Take my life; it is yours—100 percent!" Perhaps it was in a quiet moment of personal devotional study when you opened the Word and God spoke in a clear way. You were moved to say, "From this day on, I will serve you and use my gifts to further the work of your kingdom."

2

In light of Jeremiah 1:4–10, 17–19, how does God view Jeremiah, and how does Jeremiah view himself?

3

Tell about a time when you felt God's calling on your life and you were moved to offer yourself fully to him.

Read: Jeremiah 20:1–2, 7–8; 37:15–16, 20

FACING HARD DAYS

Jeremiah has some very bad days in his life and ministry. It's one thing when your ministry doesn't go along very well—people aren't responsive, there aren't breakthroughs, and there aren't miraculous answers to prayer. It is entirely another thing when you take a physical beating and face public shame just for doing what God has called you to do. For Jeremiah, this kind of abuse is a regular occurrence.

Like Jeremiah, all who follow Jesus and seek to obey his calling will discover that there are hard days along the way. Some may face only a few days of pain, sorrow, and rejection related to their commitment to follow the Savior. Others may experience far more difficult times. But everyone who commits to following God's plan for their life can plan on facing some time of sorrow, heartache, and struggle.

Jeremiah follows God faithfully, but he still faces very difficult times. What are some of the painful experiences Jeremiah endures?

4

How can facing times of suffering actually deepen and strengthen our faith?

5

> **N**othing is really lost by a life of sacrifice; everything is lost by a failure to obey God's call.
>
> **HENRY PARRY LIDDEN**

HANGING IN THERE

Jeremiah's relentless preaching seems to make no impact on the people of Judah. They refuse to listen to his warnings. Sadly, just as Jeremiah prophesies, the Babylonian army attacks and conquers Jerusalem. They destroy the city, break down the walls, and burn the temple. The people of Judah are taken into captivity as prisoners of war.

Jeremiah could look at all he has suffered—the humiliations, beatings, intimidation, and imprisonment—and feel as if it has accomplished nothing. He could also look at all the hours of preaching, waiting on the Lord, and interacting with the nation of Judah as a waste of time.

In the same way, we can get discouraged when we are trying to accomplish God's purposes and face resistance. We can feel as if our devotion and faithfulness have yielded nothing. But, like Jeremiah, we must learn that God does not measure success the same way we do. Our faithfulness in following his leading matters to God, even if we don't see the fruit of our work. We also need to have confidence that God sees the impact of our lives with a wide-angle lens. God saw the impact of Jeremiah's life even if no one else did. In the same way, we can trust that God will use our lives even when we cannot see the results immediately.

6   Tell about a hard assignment that you have right now.

7   How can your small group members pray for you and support you as you seek to honor God by working on this assignment?

MESSY PRAYER

Jeremiah is disillusioned, frustrated, and angry. He doesn't know what to do with all of his hurt. He might be tempted to put on a happy face, pretend it doesn't bother him, or even quit. But instead of these more common responses, Jeremiah does something few God-fearing people have the courage to do: He spills his guts to God.

In the midst of his pain, Jeremiah lifts up one of the messiest prayers recorded in all of Scripture. It is the kind of prayer that few people have the courage to lift up before a holy God. But Jeremiah prays—and it is recorded in Scripture for our sake. God is not afraid of honesty. He can handle authentic prayers lifted from the depth of our pain. As a matter of fact, he welcomes these prayers.

Read: Jeremiah 20:7–18

In this prayer Jeremiah ranges from the heights of trust and praise to the depths of sorrow and discouragement. What words capture the breadth of his prayer here? `8`

Respond to *one* of the following statements about prayer: `9`

- Prayer is meant exclusively for praise and worship; mourning or expressing anger in prayer is not appropriate for God's people.
- God welcomes every prayer, no matter how messy and no matter what we are feeling.

What can stand in the way of our being totally honest when we pray? `10`

What helps you grow more honest and transparent in your prayer?

> **B**ut we have this treasure in jars of clay to show that this all-surpassing power is from God and not from us. We are hard pressed on every side, but not crushed; perplexed, but not in despair; persecuted, but not abandoned; struck down, but not destroyed. We always carry around in our body the death of Jesus, so that the life of Jesus may also be revealed in our body.
>
> **THE APOSTLE PAUL (2 CORINTHIANS 4:7–10)**

Closing Reflection

Take a few minutes of silence for personal reflection . . .

Every follower of Christ will face times of struggle and discouragement. Even when we are obedient and faithful, hard times come. Think about some of the hard assignments you have faced in life and identify how God has carried you through them. If you are still in the middle of a difficult time, think about how God has been with you.

Take time to respond to this closing question . . .

What can help us experience God's presence more fully when we are in the middle of a hard assignment?

Close your small group by praying together . . .

Take time to pray for those who are walking the road of Jeremiah. Pray for strength that they may stand strong. Pray also for them to have eyes to see that God is with them, even when the road is hard. Here are some possible prayer directions for your small group:

- For those who are standing strong as they face a hard assignment, lift up prayer for strength and for a sense of God's pleasure over their faithfulness.

- For those who feel as if they are not fulfilling God's call, pray for grace and a renewed commitment to get back in the game.

- For those who are in a time of joy-filled harvest in life and ministry, pray that they may keep balance in their life and persistence in ministry without becoming proud.

Old Testament Life Challenge

DOING MINISTRY EVEN WHEN IT'S TOUGH

There are some ministries that are especially challenging. These places of service demand a certain kind of attitude and commitment. Often, those who serve in these ministries do so with little praise or affirmation. Certain ministries are critical and important to the heart of God, but often they are done in the shadows, far from the spotlight and praise of people. Pray about volunteering to do some kind of ministry, at least once a year, that demands commitment and sacrifice. Some options might be:

- ministries of compassion and calling on the sick

- set-up and take-down

- parking attendants

- nursery caregivers

- ministry to those who are uniquely challenged

- children's ministry

- work with the homeless

The Life-Giving Power of Hope

Introduction

The term "hitting bottom" has become popularized when speaking of individuals who have come to their lowest point in life (often because of addictions) and finally have nowhere to look but up. God's people in the Old Testament hit their bottom when the Babylonians invade and the nation goes into exile. Earlier in 722 B.C. the northern kingdom had been invaded by Assyria and was conquered. In 586 B.C. Jerusalem, the capital of the southern kingdom, falls. Everything seems hopeless.

Yet, out of the ashes of judgment, hope begins to arise. Even as the exiles are being sent to Babylon, a message of hope is being proclaimed. God's judgment is not just punitive, it is also redemptive. God's plan is to gather a faithful remnant and restore his people. After seventy years of exile God will give a new beginning, a fresh start, a future filled with hope.

Looking at Life

Tell about a time when someone you know went through a deep valley but came out the other side more in love with God and filled with stronger hope.

1

Learning from the Word
Read: 2 Kings 25:1-12

EXILE

Exile meant forced relocation. It meant that you'd leave your home forever. A superpower would conquer a country and give most of the population a choice: Move or die. This was how the superpowers made sure that people wouldn't try to rebel and recapture their homeland. This happened to the northern kingdom in 722 B.C. and to the southern kingdom in 586 B.C.

For nations in those days, exile was the end. Humanly speaking, the idea of coming back to one's homeland after a time of exile was not even an option. People who went into exile knew what to expect. They would eventually blend in with the other peoples of the ancient world, and their story, their culture, their language, and their faith would all disappear.

2

In the eleventh year of King Zedekiah, on the ninth day of the fourth month, everything in Jerusalem changed. How do you think Zedekiah would describe what happened on that fateful day?

If you met King Nebuchadnezzar right after the events recorded in 2 Kings 25, how do you think he would describe what had happened?

3

Imagine the conquest that is recorded in this passage happening today. It was your capital city that fell and your national leader that was subdued, and you were part of the group of people taken into exile. How would your life be changed?

How might your faith in God be impacted?

Read: Jeremiah 29:1–14

THE HEART OF JEREMIAH

Jeremiah writes a letter to the exiles in Babylon. These are the very people he warned year after year. They are the ones to whom Jeremiah had come with God's call to repentance over and over. These are the people who had refused to listen to anything the prophet said.

Imagine for a moment that you were Jeremiah. You have preached the truth and your audience had turned on you. They laughed at you. They mocked you. They didn't believe you. They threw you into prison. They carted you off to Egypt. Then, exactly what you warned them about comes true. Now, you write a letter to the very people who mocked you all those years. What tone would your letter have? What would be the condition of your heart?

For most of us, we would be filled with anger and even righteous indignation. For Jeremiah, his heart was still tender. Although he has to deal with the reality of judgment and exile, he also speaks of hope and restoration and gives practical advice about how to live in their new land. Jeremiah shows a level of tenderness that most of us find unthinkable in this setting.

What is God's advice for his people as they go into exile in Babylon?   **4**

Why do you think God calls his people to these specific actions while they are in exile?   **5**

Read: Jeremiah 29:4–7; Ezra 1:1–11

PRAYING FOR BABYLON

In his letter to the exiles in Babylon, Jeremiah calls them to settle in. They should try to establish a normal life there. He wants them to build homes, plant gardens, get married, have children, and establish themselves in the new land. Beyond that, Jeremiah says: "Also, seek the peace and prosperity of the city to which I have carried you into exile. *Pray to the LORD for it,* because if it prospers, you too will prosper" (Jeremiah 29:7).

The whole idea seems counterintuitive. Why pray for Babylon? This is the nation that has conquered them. These are the people that have destroyed Jerusalem, their holy city. Babylon is the ever-present reminder that they are strangers in a strange land. But God calls them, through the prophet Jeremiah, to pray for the prosperity of Babylon!

6 The natural inclination for God's people may have been to pray for the fall and destruction of Babylon. However, God calls for them to do just the opposite. If you were one of the people of Israel, what kind of prayer do you think you would have lifted up for Babylon and the leaders of this nation?

7 God wants his people to pray for those who are in positions of authority (including national leaders). What are some specific prayers you believe followers of Christ should be lifting up for your nation and your leaders?

Read: Jeremiah 29:10–14

A NEW TIME AND A NEW DREAM

Long ago Israel had hoped to become a superpower like Babylon or Assyria. But by this time in their history it has become painfully apparent that this dream will never come to pass. Israel will never see a mighty king lead them to win great battles, they will never again possess enormous wealth, and the hope of conquering new lands is no longer on their national radar. These dreams are dead. Thankfully, the people have finally realized that these are the wrong dreams. They are foolish dreams. They aren't God's dreams for his people, and they never have been.

A few among them are beginning to dream a new dream. God births in them a new vision. They realize that what looks like the end can be a beginning. Maybe they will finally become a community that will be great in the sight of God. Some begin to believe and understand that the greatness God wants to birth in them is not about armies, power, wealth, or things that make them look impressive in the eyes of the world. Greatness is based on turning their hearts toward God and humbly following him. From the beginning God has a dream of building a new community of people who love him, each other, and the world. Finally, it seems that this dream is beginning to come alive in the hearts of God's people.

8

The message from God recorded in Jeremiah 29 comes at the lowest point in their national history. Their bitter enemy has conquered them. The holy city Jerusalem has fallen. They have been taken to Babylon as prisoners of war. Right in the middle of this devastation, we read these words: "'For I know the plans I have for you,' declares the LORD, 'plans to prosper you and not to harm you, plans to give you a hope and a future'" (Jeremiah 29:11). How can these words make any sense in light of what they are experiencing?

9

In Jeremiah 29:10–14 God is specific about what he plans to do. What does God promise he will do and why might this bring hope to the people in captivity?

10

Tell about a time God brought you hope in a situation that others may have seen as hopeless.

Closing Reflection

Take a few minutes of silence for personal reflection . . .

The people of Judah are facing a time of judgment and suffering unparalleled in their national history. How do you think you would have responded if you were one of them?

Take time to respond to these closing questions . . .

> *How does hope in God's promises help carry us through the hard times we face?*

The Bible is full of promises God has given to those who follow him.

> *What is one biblical promise that gives you hope and encouragement in the difficult times of life?*

Close your small group by praying together . . .
Take time to pray for the following:

- Pray for people who are walking through a painful and difficult time in their life.

- Ask God to give you a heart of tenderness and compassion toward others, even toward those who have wronged you.

- Lift up your nation and your national leaders.

- Pray for the hope of God to fill your hearts, even during times that feel hopeless.

Old Testament Life Challenge

THE HEART OF JESUS

God wants all of his children to live with humble hearts. The more we yield to him, the more he can use us. Jesus is an example of complete humility and submission to the Father. It was Jesus who said: "My Father, if it is possible, may this cup be taken from me. Yet not as I will, but as you will" (Matthew 26:39). As Jesus faced the cross, he affirmed his full submission to the Father by saying three times that he would not seek his own will but the will of the Father. It is this same spirit that must come alive in the lives of Christ's followers today if we are going to realize God's dream for our lives.

The exile of the nation of Judah brought them to a place of humble submission. They hit bottom and had nowhere to look but up—to God. They refused to say, "Your will be done," until they hit bottom. We don't have to wait that long.

Learn from the lesson of Judah. If there is an area of your life that God has been calling you to repent, hear his call and respond! Echo the words of Jesus and say, "Not as I will, but as you will." Don't wait until you hit bottom, but freely confess today and ask God for power to change the way you are living.

OTC

LEADER'S NOTES

CONTENTS

Elijah: Holding Steady in a Roller Coaster World

THE HEART
of a Leader

Elijah is an amazing example of holding steady in a roller coaster world. He had times of astounding victory in his life when he saw the power of God pour down from heaven. He also had times of deep fear, insecurity, and even depression. He rode the roller coaster of life and faith and held on with all his might.

As you prepare to lead this small group, take time to reflect on where you are in your life. Maybe you are in a season of joy, peace, and confident faith. Maybe you are discouraged and you feel like you are holding on for dear life. Maybe you are in the depths of depression and sadness. Wherever you are, God wants to speak to your heart and teach you about holding steady in your faith through this amazing ride we call life. God used Elijah to accomplish his purposes when he felt weak and when he felt strong, and God can use you to lead this life-changing small group right where you are today.

THE PRAYER
of a Leader

In this life, we will have moments of great joy and intense sorrow. We will experience times of deep faith when God feels close and we see his power. We will also walk through valley times of confusion and darkness when God seems distant and removed. No matter what we face in this roller coaster life, we can hold steady because God is always with us, even when our eyes can't see him and our hearts can't feel him. Take time in prayer to ask God to meet each person in your small group right where they are. Pray for group members, including yourself, to be honest and vulnerable as you begin this study.

Questions 2–3

When the drought devastates the land and the stream dries up, God sends Elijah to a widow to be fed. At first glance, this may not seem strange, but in those days widows were the poorest and most vulnerable members of society. Because of the place of women in general, and widows in specific, these were usually very poor people who were often outcasts. Yet, God chooses to use a poor widow to provide for his prophet.

Not only is this woman a poor widow, she is also from Sidon. This is Jezebel's hometown, which means the woman is most likely a pagan. But God sees and God cares for this pagan widow and for his prophet, Elijah.

The story is powerful and dramatic because when Elijah meets this woman and asks if she will feed him, she informs him that her situation is so desperate that her plan for that day is to make one final meal for her and her son and then to die of starvation! Just think about it. She has two items to check off her "To Do" list for the day:

- Fix a meal
- Die

Yet Elijah gives her hope. He assures her that if she takes what little food remains and prepares a meal for him, she will still have enough for her and her son. Beyond that, Elijah lets her know that God will provide miraculous resources for them every day until the drought is over. And what Elijah promises comes to pass. Every time she uses the flour and oil, there is more in the containers for the next day.

Their hopeless situation is turned upside down by God's surprising provision. Who would have dreamed that a pagan widow on the edge of poverty and starvation would be the one to have enough faith to give her final meal to a traveling prophet? Who would have dreamed that each day the jars would remain full of oil and flour? But this is just like God—his provision is often a mystery, but always enough.

The key phrase in the story of Elijah and the widow is when Elijah says, "But first." God's question of this widow is, "Will you trust me now with what you have?" Here is a lesson about human nature: *If you won't trust God now with what you have, you won't trust him when you get more.*

WORD STUDY: SYNCRETISM

Syncretism is the effort to embrace various religious systems at the same time. In the Old Testament, we see this practice when God's people try to retain the practice of worshiping Yahweh, the God who revealed himself to Abraham, Isaac, and Jacob, along with adopting the religions of the nations around them. In many cases, it appears as if the people really believe they can do both—hold onto worship of Yahweh with one hand and Baal with the other. They try to adopt the religious practices and worship the idols of the Canaanites and other nations and still maintain their distinct worship of Yahweh.

Questions 4–5

Elijah tells Ahab what to do. He has him gather the people from all over Israel to meet on Mount Carmel so that they can settle this issue of religious syncretism once and for all. Elijah tells the king to bring all of the false prophets that Jezebel has set up in places of authority all over the land. This includes 450 prophets of Baal and 400 prophets of Asherah. All of these 850 are sponsored and supported by Jezebel. Ahab does exactly as Elijah commands.

We have to picture this amazing scene on Mount Carmel. People from all over Israel have gathered. The 850 false prophets are there, and then Elijah shows up. The whole country is gathered for this moment. On one side stand all the false prophets, the king, and all the power of his government and his army. On Ahab's side is the absolute license for the people to do whatever they feel like. There are no Ten Commandments there. There is no law about caring for orphans, widows, and aliens. There is no call for devotion to love God and neighbor. It's just idolatry that promises sexual pleasure as part of the cult worship and material abundance for all who bow down to Baal.

On the other side stands one man, one solitary prophet who emerges from years of hiding to confront a king and a country. But with that one man is God—Israel's God—the God who made them a people. The God of Abraham, Isaac, Jacob, and Joseph is with Elijah. Standing with Elijah is the God who delivers meals by ravens and who fills the oil and flour jars of widows. To the naked eye, it seems as if Elijah is outnumbered 850 to 1. But to the spiritual eye, Elijah is far from alone!

Standing in the middle are the people of Israel. They are at their critical deciding point. They have tried holding on to both Yahweh and Baal. They have been living syncretistic lives. But now, a line is being drawn.

In an act of immense courage, Elijah challenges a whole nation. He cries out the question that has been burning in the heart of God. Elijah stands before the people and says, "How long will you waver between two opinions? If the LORD is God, follow him; but if Baal is God, follow him."

Why is Elijah saying the people are wavering between two opinions? They don't think they have rejected Yahweh. They still pray to him if nothing else works. They just think they have added Baal to their religious portfolio. They have decided they'll worship both. The word translated "waver" here literally means "to hobble" or "to limp."

The Hebrews often used "walking" as a metaphor for life. Elijah is saying, "You are just limping through life. You have chosen a miserable way to live. You are being torn between two gods, and one of them is false." This image of limping speaks as loudly today as it did in the days of

Elijah. When a person tries to follow the one true God and still embrace false gods, they will never walk securely, and they will certainly never run—they will limp along!

WORD STUDY: ELIJAH

Elijah's name is made up of two parts. "Jah" comes from Yahweh and "El" from Elohim. His name actually means, "The LORD [Yahweh] is Elohim." In other words, "The LORD is God." That's what Elijah's name means. What is interesting is that his name also expresses his life mission—to declare that Yahweh, and Yahweh alone, is God!

THE "NATURE GOD"

Baal was said to be the god of nature. He is pictured in ancient etchings with lightning bolts in his hand. The ancient writings said that Baal rode the thunderstorm as his chariot. In other words, a little fire from heaven should have been a piece of cake for Baal. If he really did exist, sending fire from heaven was in his job description! Since Baal was known as the "Nature God," the people would have seen this challenge as an easy task for him.

Questions 6–7

Nobody stays on top of the mountain forever—nobody. We will all have spiritual peaks and valleys as long as we live. Sometimes, after an unbelievable, adrenaline-filled, record-setting run of achievement and spiritual victory, we can find ourselves in the most vulnerable times of doubt, fear, or depression. The question is not, "Will I ever visit the valley?" The real issue is, "How will I respond when I do visit the valley?"

Elijah is about to snap. The same Elijah who prayed and fire came down from heaven to consume a sacrifice, who prayed for rain and a drought was ended, who received the strength to outrun a chariot, prays for one more thing: "Let me die." But the good news is that God loves Elijah too much to answer the words of this prayer. He is so down that he does not know how he can press on, yet God still has a plan for Elijah. God hears Elijah's honest and passionate prayer. The prophet tells God exactly how he feels. Elijah prays from the depths, God hears from the heights, and God prepares to lift Elijah out of the pit he is in.

In his book *Out of the Depths*, Bernhard W. Anderson addresses this issue of honesty in prayer. He sees the honest prayers of the Old Testament lifted from a place of pain, but always with a sense of confidence that God will lift up the prayer and bring deliverance. As he writes about the psalms of lament, he says:

The lament is an appeal to God's compassion to intervene and change a desperate situation . . . they raise a cry out of the depths in the confidence that God has the power to lift a person out of the "miry bog" and set one's feet upon a rock. Hence the laments are really expressions of praise—praise offered in a minor key in the confidence that Yahweh is faithful and in anticipation of a new lease on life.

Questions 8–10

When Elijah reaches the Negev, at least geographically, he has left the people of Israel. He is far from God's people. In a sense, he has left his post. That's why God says, "What are you doing here?" Elijah is running away from what God has for him to do. He has classic signs of depression: suicidal thoughts, loss of appetite, and a distorted perspective on reality.

You can bet that inside Elijah's mind a little voice is saying things like, "You call yourself a prophet? You have more doubt and fear than the people you preach to. You ran out on God after all he did for you. You left the people just when they started turning from Baal and needed you most. There's no way God could ever use somebody like you."

Elijah must have felt like we all do on some days. He must have had a sense that he was not useful for God's purposes and that his future was pretty bleak. But God had news for him. His life matters and his ministry is still needed. God gives Elijah a new vision and a fresh calling. What began as a sad scene ends up joy-filled and hopeful.

LEADER'S NOTES

Elijah: Receiving a Spiritual Legacy

THE HEART
of a Leader

In this session we will look at how God called Elijah to pass on the flame of faith to the next generation. His flame was given to Elisha, and he, in turn, continued to pass it on. In a similar way, followers of Christ today are invited into the joy-filled experience of investing their lives and faith in another generation of believers. It might be a class of children taught during a Sunday school hour. It could be high school students in a youth group that receive the flame. For many it will be their sons and daughters and grandchildren. There are also those who will become spiritual sons and daughters, much like Elisha became a spiritual son to Elijah. Whoever it is, God calls us to be ready to invest our lives in passing the torch of faith to the next generation and leaving a spiritual legacy.

Take time to reflect in two different directions as you prepare to bring this message. First, think about those who have passed on the flame of faith to you over the years. Thank God for their lives and faithfulness. Next, think about those whom God has placed in your life and to whom he has called you to pass on the torch. Pray for boldness, consistency, and wisdom as you continue to follow God's leading in passing on a spiritual legacy to others.

THE PRAYER
of a Leader

Ask God to move in your heart on two levels as you prepare to lead this small group. First, ask God to bring to your memory many people who have had an influence on your faith journey. Second, invite the Spirit to help you identify people to whom you should be passing the flame. Prepare yourself to be used by God in the lives of these people.

Questions 2–3

When Elijah was on the mountain, God spoke to him. He was discouraged, and in despair he poured his heart out to God. Right in the middle of this low point in Elijah's life, God lets him know that he is not done passing on his flame. There is a man named Elisha who needs the leadership Elijah has to offer. God lets Elijah know that he will be grooming Elisha to be the new prophet in Israel.

In 1 Kings 19:15–16 God tells Elijah that he will be anointing two kings. Then God slips in, "And by the way, you will also be anointing your replacement." How do you think Elijah feels when he hears those words? It takes a certain kind of humility to do what Elijah is called to do.

Up to this point, Elijah has been the key prophet for God in Israel. When you are a prophet, you tend to get a certain amount of attention and your role carries a certain measure of power. God informs Elijah that he will be giving up his place as the number one prophet in the land. Elijah must acknowledge that a younger man will take over for him. He has to face the reality that a new prophet will take his place and that Elisha may even go farther than Elijah did.

When Elisha decides to follow Elijah, this is a significant event in his life. It needs to be acknowledged and even celebrated. So, a big party takes place. What we have recorded is a brief account of something that would have taken a considerable amount of time to plan. A huge celebration takes place. The word "huge" might not really hit the mark. Look at it this way: Have you ever seen a side of beef? Can you imagine how many people you can feed with *two* oxen? Oxen are big animals. Elisha's family has an enormous feast to celebrate this step in his life. They affirm his decision.

We must learn from this example in our homes, relationships, and churches. When people say yes to a volunteer place of ministry, it is a big deal! When somebody says, "Yes, I will! I don't have to do it, I have other options, but I'm going to devote myself to the task God has placed before me," this deserves celebration!

It is important, in the life of the church, to make time to rejoice over those who are serving God as volunteers. We need to have a barbecue, throw a party, publicly bless and pray for people, and do all we can to celebrate those who follow God's example of being a volunteer.

A RICH KID

When Elijah comes to Elisha and invites him to follow in the steps of the prophet, it will involve great commitment and sacrifice on the part of Elisha. Take note of the number of oxen Elisha is plowing with. In that day, most families were poor enough that they might own a few chickens. For a family to own one ox was rare and a sign of wealth. They'd be fairly well off. To have twelve teams of oxen (twenty-four) was almost unheard of. It indicates that Elisha's family is incredibly wealthy. In contemporary terms, they have a huge house in the wealthiest neighborhood in town and a condo in Maui. Elisha is a rich kid, no question about it!

W hen volunteers are asked how they happened to get involved in their particular activity, the most common answer is, "Somebody asked me." When people are asked why they did not volunteer or donate, they say, "Nobody asked."

ROBERT PUTNAM

Questions 4–5

Elijah and Elisha begin their journey in Gilgal, which is close to the Jordan River. Elijah tells Elisha to stay there while he goes on to Bethel. But Elisha said, "As surely as the LORD lives and as you live, I will not leave you." This is a strong response from Elisha. He lets Elijah know, "Nothing doing. I'm going to stick with you." So, Elijah moves on and Elisha goes with him.

Next, they go to Bethel, which is quite a way inland. It is almost halfway to the Mediterranean Sea. Once they are in Bethel, they go through the same set of speeches. Elijah tells him to wait there, and Elisha is emphatic that he is not leaving Elijah's side.

So, they travel to Jericho. In Jericho they echo the same conversation and move on. Finally, they end up at the Jordan River. This seems like a strange journey, and the recurring conversation between these two prophets can seem odd. But, the issue at hand seems to be a test to see if Elisha is fully committed to following Elijah, and ultimately, following God.

We don't know exactly why Elijah keeps telling Elisha to stay behind. Maybe Elijah wants to face the end alone. Maybe he's afraid what he is going to experience will be too much for Elisha to handle. Maybe it is a test to see if Elisha proves to be a follower of unshakable loyalty. No matter what the reason, the result is clear to see. Elisha is so committed to following his mentor that he proves a level of loyalty that is tenacious and unshakable. Like a bulldog with his teeth locked onto a steak, Elisha won't let go of his mentor and friend.

Not only is there no jealousy or rivalry between these men, there is deep affection and God-honoring friendship. When the torch is passed the right way, it can create extraordinary oneness and community.

Finally the two of them come to the Jordan River. They know their time together is short. Elijah takes off his mantle—the same one he spread over Elisha so long ago—wraps it up, and strikes the river. Just as the water separated a long time ago for Joshua (and for Moses at the Red Sea), now it separates for Elijah.

Elijah and Elisha cross over together on dry ground. They leave the Promised Land, the ordinary world, for an extraordinary event. At this decisive moment Elijah does a wonderful thing. He is about to leave this world and Elisha's side. But he doesn't give a lot of advice, instructions, or commands. Elijah simply asks Elisha one last question.

Like all great questions, this one is a little bit of a test. It's a little like when God asked Solomon, "What do you want if I could give you anything?" Elijah asks Elisha, "What can I do for you before I am taken from you?" What a great question! This is a question that every torch-passer should learn to ask: "What can I do for you?"

Questions 6–7

Elisha encounters a woman who is in dire straits. Her sons are about to be sold into slavery. She is deeply in debt and has nowhere to go and no one to help her. So, she runs to Elisha. This woman is sure she has nothing of any value. But Elisha asks a provocative question. He asks the woman if she has *anything at all* in her house. Her response is, "Your servant has nothing there at all except a little oil."

Elisha tells her that God will miraculously give all the oil she needs so she can sell it and pay off all her debts. His words bring hope that she and her sons will have all they need to live. But Elisha first asks her to do something specific. She must gather as many jars as she can find. She is to go around to all of her neighbors and ask for every container they can spare. Elisha speaks these words: "Don't ask for just a few."

Questions 8–10

The king of Aram is trying to kill the king of Israel, and he makes many attempts to assassinate Joram. But every time he makes a plan, God tells Elisha, who passes the information on to the king of Israel. So, every time the king of Aram advances, Joram escapes.

The king of Aram starts to get angry. He can't figure out why the king of Israel is always one step ahead of him. Thus, the king of Aram starts to ask some questions, "Who's the mole? Where's the leak? How can Joram know my plans before I execute them?" He is sure there is someone in his camp that is working as a double agent.

His leaders assure him that there is not a mole. They tell him that Elisha has the power to know the very words the king speaks in the privacy of his own bedroom. The king of Aram decides that the only way he will ever get to King Joram is to take out Elisha first. So, again, a prophet of God finds out what it is like to be on the death list of a king.

The king of Aram finds out that Elisha has gone to the city of Dothan, so he brings in his army and surrounds the city. They are there for one reason—to capture and terminate Elisha. Just think about it, one man demands the attack of a whole army.

I have learned to place myself before God every day as a vessel to be filled with His Holy Spirit. He has filled me with the blessed assurance that He, as the everlasting God, has guaranteed His own work in me.

ANDREW MURRAY

I am the LORD your God, who brought you up out of Egypt. Open wide your mouth and I will fill it.

PSALM 81:10

The next morning Elisha's servant gets up and looks outside of the city. There is a human wall surrounding the city on every side. There are soldiers, chariots, and a military machine that would send fear into the heart of any ordinary man. But Elisha is not an ordinary man, because he serves an extraordinary God. When Elisha's servant looks and sees their situation, all he can see is the apparent power and impenetrable position of the army surrounding the city. When Elisha looks, he sees something very different. Elisha says to his servant: "Don't be afraid. . . . Those who are with us are more than those who are with them" (2 Kings 6:16).

How do you think Elisha's words sound to his servant as he looks and sees the army surrounding the city? You can almost hear him saying, "How many are with us? Two." And then looking outside the city again and saying, "How many are with them? I can't count that high!" He must wonder what Elisha is talking about. How can Elisha say that those who are with them are more than the ones who surround the city?

Then Elisha prays for God to open his servant's eyes and help him see beyond the physical world to the spiritual reality. When God opens the eyes of Elijah's servant, he sees a radically different reality. The hills all around Dothan are full of horses and chariots of fire. The army of God surrounds the army of Aram, and they also surround Elisha. Human eyes show that the odds are in favor of the king of Aram. Spiritual eyes reveal that the King of heaven is with Elisha, and the victory always goes to God!

There is a postscript to the story of Elisha's servant learning that "those who are with us are more than those who are with them." Elisha prays for God to blind the entire army. Once they are blind, Elisha leads them into the capital city of Israel. This is the hometown of King Joram, whom the king of Aram has been plotting to kill. Once they are in the city and surrounded by the army of Israel, God opens their eyes and they realize they are in big trouble.

The king of Israel asks Elisha if he should execute the entire army. Elisha says, "I have a better idea! Let's have them sit down and let's serve them a feast!" And that is exactly what they do. Elisha exercises shocking compassion and grace. The postscript to the postscript is that the army of Aram stops raiding and harassing the people of Israel. Is that any surprise?

LEADER'S NOTES

Amos: How to Measure a Life

THE HEART
of a Leader

In a critical time of Israel's history, God spoke through Amos to give the people a serious wake-up call. The time of Amos's ministry was one of great affluence and peace. Not since the days of Solomon could the people remember a time when things were going so well in their nation. The economy was strong, and those who were rich just seemed to be getting richer! It seemed everyone was reaping the benefits of this season of God's blessing—everyone except the poor.

As we read the book of Amos, it quickly becomes apparent that the rich were indeed getting richer. But at the same time, the poor were getting poorer and, in some ways, the wealth of the rich was being amassed at the expense of the poor and through unjust practices.

God calls Amos to speak to the nation. He calls them to justice, righteousness, and compassion. God is deeply concerned for the plight of all who are marginalized, and he calls his people to adopt a new attitude and lifestyle that reflect his care for the poor and oppressed.

This message has a great deal to say to those who live in affluence. The warnings and exhortations from Amos echo through the millennia and speak to the church and followers of Christ in our day. If we listen closely, we can hear the call from complacency to acts of justice and compassion. Let this message hit deep in your heart as you prepare to lead your small group. Invite the Spirit to search your heart and reveal any place where injustice is hiding.

THE PRAYER
of a Leader

Anyone who lives in an affluent society can be tempted to consume more and express less compassion with each passing year. Many followers of Jesus need to do a close lifestyle examination to be sure that they are living with a generous spirit, a heart of compassion, and eyes that are always open to the needs of the poor and the outcast. As a small group leader, pray for every member of your small group to have a soft heart to receive what God wants to say. When it comes to sensitive topics like the ones in this session, it is easy to get defensive and refuse to listen. Pray that every

LEADER'S NOTES

member of your small group will come ready to hear, learn, and let God change their heart.

Question 1

Amos lived and ministered around 750 B.C. He was *not* a professional prophet. He was a farmer. He took care of a few sheep and tended some fig trees. He was from a little town near Bethlehem called Tekoa, in the southern kingdom (Judah). One day, God calls this man to leave his sheep and go proclaim God's word. God does not call Amos to preach in Judah, his hometown, but God tells him to go up to the northern kingdom (Israel) and preach there. Right from the start Amos is going to have to be bold. He is going to preach to the nation that has been in a civil war with his people for many years.

Questions 2–4

Every society and generation must face the reality that there are groups that can be easily marginalized. In the days of Amos it is the alien, the orphan, and the widow. Our responsibility is to discern where these groups exist in our society and then seek to extend the compassion and tender love of God for these people. We must seek justice for those who are often treated with injustice. The particular groups of people may change with varied contexts, but there will always be marginalized people groups, and God will always expect his children to seek them out and extend justice and mercy toward them.

The marginalized could be persons of color, senior citizens, teenagers, people with physical or mental disabilities, or some minority group, but every society has them. It is so important that we understand the heart of God toward these people and take actions that communicate his love for the outcasts.

God says he will judge a society by the way it treats marginalized people. God makes it unmistakably clear that he takes it on himself to be the protector of the weak and outcast ones in a society. He makes it unmistakably clear that anybody who neglects them neglects him. Anybody who oppresses them oppresses him.

ALIEN, ORPHANS, AND WIDOWS

Why is God so concerned for these three groups of people? *Aliens* are those who have immigrated into the land of Israel. They are not ethnic Israelites so they do not have the same rights and privileges as the people of Israel. *Orphans* are those who have no one to provide for them or to look out for them. *Widows* are women who have lost their husband and in the patriarchal society in which they live, they are without power or economic means.

In our day these would be called marginalized people. They are the groups who will most likely be forgotten, mistreated, oppressed, and broken if someone does not speak up. God is concerned for these groups because they need someone to help them, to speak for them, to love them.

Questions 5–7

We live in a society that often encourages us to live like cows of Bashan. Our media culture wants us to become walking appetites for money, food, and pleasure. "How can I get a bigger house?" "How can I get a larger income?" "How can I drive a newer car?" "How can I have greater sexual pleasure?" "How can I be more attractive?" Our culture has become very effective in producing cows of Bashan. This reality should cause every follower of Jesus to evaluate their lives and motives closely.

The deeper problem for the people of Israel was that they have made no connection between their treatment of the poor and their relationship with God. We can fall into this same pattern. We can worship, give our offerings, and feel pretty good about ourselves, but our hearts might still be hard toward those who are poor and outcast. God wants to touch our hearts and help us feel as he does for the poor. Then, he wants to transform our lifestyles and teach us to be generous toward the marginalized and needy.

Amos hits the people of Israel right where they live. He lets them know that God sees their greed and devaluation of human life. To many of these people a human life is worth as much as a pair of sandals. In many cases, they value a pair of their shoes *more* than a person.

Over time, many of the people became so wealthy that they built winter and summer homes. They invested all their money in creating luxurious places to live, and they have nothing left to give to the poor. God lets the people know that their opulent lifestyle and hard hearts will lead to their downfall. God speaks through Amos and says, "I will tear down the winter house along with the summer house; the houses adorned with ivory will be destroyed and the mansions will be demolished."

Questions 8–10

Imagine the shock waves going through the crowd when they hear Amos claiming that God says he hates their worship and religious observance. They have never heard such a thing. What can this mean?

LEADER'S NOTES

God is saying to the people, "Your worship and your lives cannot be separated!" They want to hoard wealth, trample on the poor, and oppress the weak and then show up for church as if God does not notice any of their behavior. God is clear that life does not work this way. Injustice and authentic worship cannot coexist in the life of someone who follows Jesus.

LEADER'S NOTES

THE HEART
of a Leader

God invites Isaiah into a staggering place of worship. Isaiah sees God and is never the same. He learns that true and authentic worship has a price tag. It will cost a man or woman all they have and all they are. When we see God in the glory of his holiness, we enter worship as it was meant to be.

No more halfhearted songs, sleepy prayers, and leftovers in the offering plate. The radiance of God's holiness invites us to place our hearts and lives on the altar and echo the words of Isaiah, "Here am I. Send me!" Take time to examine your own patterns in worship. Are you fully engaged when you worship? Are there distractions to worshiping God that you need to remove from your life?

THE PRAYER
of a Leader

We will never learn spiritual authenticity until we come to the throne of God. In the light of his holiness, all pretense, facades, and playacting melt away. We learn to be authentic, who we really are, before God's throne.

As you prepare to lead this small group, spend time at the throne of God. Speak with him in prayer. Sing to him. Meditate on his Word. Meet with God and ask the Holy Spirit to remove any attitudes or actions that are inauthentic. Ask God to help you see his holiness and transform you through his presence.

Question 1

The costly nature of worship goes beyond the investment we make to be sure we show up and gather with others for a worship service. There is a deeper cost when we decide to worship God. In worship we give the gift of concentrating sustained attention on God. We seek to authentically bring the fullness of our emotional life before God as we worship. We submit to follow the leading and prompting he gives through our worship experience. Worship always costs something.

LEADER'S NOTES

Questions 2–3

Uzziah reigned for a long time. If you do a study of the kings of Israel and Judah, you quickly discover that some of them had short runs as king. But Uzziah ruled in Jerusalem for fifty-two years. Try to get your mind around what it would feel like for an American to have a leader in office for fifty-two years.

To put this into context, think about how many men have held the office of president over the past fifty-two years. To illustrate this there is a Power Point slide that lists the presidents from George W. Bush back to Harry Truman!

Most of the people of Judah can only remember one leader ruling in Jerusalem. For their whole lives, Uzziah has been on the throne. He is their anchor. He is a source of strength and confidence for the nation. He is their king.

Now Uzziah is dead. Assyria, an emerging superpower, is gobbling up little nations like Judah. The people are getting nervous. If Uzziah were on the throne, he would know what to do. But the king is dead. Uzziah is gone!

What do you do when Uzziah dies? What do you do when your anchor breaks loose and you feel as if you are cut afloat? How do you respond when the very thing you count on lets you down? What do you do when:

- you lose your job?
- your tenacity wanes?
- your money runs out?
- your rock-solid relationship begins to shake?
- everything you were counting on begins to unravel and there's no more safety net?

This is the question being asked by the people of Judah in the days of Isaiah. What do you do when Uzziah dies?

Every follower of Jesus has to ask the question: What will I do when the things I place my trust in fall apart and let me down? Where will I look?

Isaiah has learned what to do when Uzziah dies. He turns his eyes from the temporary, earthly throne of a man to the eternal throne of God! Uzziah is dead, but God is alive. The throne of Judah is empty, but the throne of heaven is occupied. The king of Judah is gone, but God will never leave. Isaiah needs to remember what we all need to learn, that there is One seated on the throne of heaven, and he reigns over the affairs of human beings.

Questions 4–5

We get a sense of the greatness of God's holiness when we see heavenly beings actually covering their faces in his presence. In light of this, we should be amazed at what Jesus says in the Sermon on the Mount. Jesus tells the people: "Blessed are the pure in heart, for they will see God" (Matthew 5:8). What a staggering reality. Through Jesus Christ we can experience cleansing from sin and a new heart. Through Jesus our hearts are made so pure that we can be confident that one day we will see God face to face. We won't have to hide our faces, wear a veil, or cover anything. We will see the holy God of heaven face to face because of the purity that is imparted to us through Jesus.

Isaiah sees these heavenly beings flying with wings covering their faces and feet. They are crying out, "Holy, holy, holy is the LORD Almighty." We may wonder why the angelic beings declare God's holiness three times. R. C. Sproul brings a great deal of clarity. He points out that in the English language we have many ways to emphasize something. If we want to get somebody's attention when we are writing, we can put the words in capital letters or italics, or we can use an exclamation mark!

Sometimes in the Bible a word gets mentioned twice in order to bring emphasis. Jesus often said, "Truly, truly." It was his way of getting the attention of those who were listening and helping them realize that what he was about to say was of the utmost importance.

On a handful of occasions a word gets repeated three times in the Bible. This elevates it to a matter of ultimate importance. Only once in the entire Bible is an attribute of God elevated to this level. It is interesting to note that God is never called, "Loving, loving, loving." He is never addressed as, "Just, just, just." Nowhere in all the Bible do we read, "Compassionate, compassionate, compassionate." Although God is absolutely loving, just, and compassionate, these attributes are never repeated three times in a row. Only the holiness of God gets the x3 symbol next to it. Holiness gets to the core of who our God is.

Questions 6–7

When Isaiah steps into the light of God's holiness, he says, "Woe to me! ... I am ruined," because he sees the true condition of his soul. His self-serving bias is gone, and he realizes that only God can remake him.

At the throne of God Isaiah sees the full extent of his ruin and darkness. The reality of his sin overwhelms him. Apart from God's grace, Isaiah would have been completely devastated. He is undone when he sees himself in the light of God's holiness. Then, the angel takes a live coal from the altar and brings it to Isaiah. Isaiah stands there and allows it to touch his lips, one of the most sensitive parts of the human body.

LEADER'S NOTES

Can you imagine what it would be like to have someone approach your mouth with a live coal? Do you think you'd just stand there? Through Isaiah we learn that there is real pain, a real sting, to the process of confession and repentance. Some people think that experiencing grace means they will never feel pain. Isaiah learns that deep grace can often mean feeling deep pain.

> My soul is like a mirror in which the glory of God is reflected, but sin, however insignificant, covers the mirror with smoke.
>
> SAINT THERESA

The goal of God's grace is *not* primarily to spare us from pain. It is to redeem our character. Experiencing remorse and sorrow over our sin is an important part of this process. If you were to ask a judge or parole board if genuine remorse matters in their decision to let a criminal go free, they will tell you that it is extremely important.

WOE

When Isaiah sees the living, holy God, his first response is not excitement. He does not celebrate that he's been singled out for something special. He does not start thinking about how he can impress other people with his amazing spiritual experience. Rather, he says, "Woe. . . ." That's an important prophetic word. It was the word the prophets used to pronounce judgment. All through the prophets the word "woe" is a flag that indicates words of judgment will follow. When Jesus spoke of God's judgment on the religious leaders of his day, he said, "Woe to you, teachers of the law and Pharisees, you hypocrites!" (Matthew 23:23, 25, 27, 29).

What is unique and unprecedented about Isaiah is that when he says "Woe," he is getting ready to pronounce judgment on himself. He says, "Woe to me! . . . I am ruined!" The prophets often said "Woe" as they spoke of God's judgment on nations, but Isaiah alone declares a "Woe" on himself. When Isaiah sees the holiness of God, it causes him to see the full extent of the darkness in his own being, and he is shattered. The true condition of the depths of his soul—his real thoughts, motives, desires, petty cruelty, and the unrelenting selfishness—becomes visible to him for the first time. He is horrified. Only one word makes sense at a moment like that: "Woe!"

Questions 8-9

Later in the book of Isaiah we get greater insight into the call of Isaiah.
We read:

> *It is too small a thing for you to be my servant*
> *to restore the tribes of Jacob*
> *and bring back those of Israel I have kept.*
> *I will also make you a light for the Gentiles,*
> *that you may bring my salvation to the ends of the earth.*
> (Isaiah 49:6)

This idea of God being a light for all the Gentiles is radical and new.
Up to this point, there were many people who were thought to be
excluded from God's love and plan. Foreigners were not thought to be
welcome, eunuchs were excluded, and many others were not invited. But
now everything is going to change. Everyone will be welcome!

Acts 8:26–39 records Philip's encounter with an Ethiopian eunuch.
This man has been excluded from Israel on multiple levels, but again we
see God's arms wide open. We see here that everyone is welcome if they
come through faith in Jesus.

In this story Philip is led by the Holy Spirit to encounter this
Ethiopian eunuch. God tells Philip, "I want this man included in my
people."

Here is a bonus question: When Philip meets this man, he is reading
from a book in the Old Testament; what book is it? It is Isaiah!

After a conversation and a time of teaching, the Holy Spirit inspires
Philip to offer baptism to this man. In a moment, through faith in Jesus,
this eunuch, who is also a foreigner, becomes part of God's family.

Jesus likewise addressed this issue of the open arms of the Father.
He said: "My house will be called a house of prayer for all nations"
(Mark 11:17).

LEADER'S NOTES

THE HEART
of a Leader

Both Ahaz and Hezekiah face fear-producing times. The difference between these men is not what life throws at them; it is how they respond when the hard times come. Ahaz folds under the force of fear. Hezekiah turns to God and walks in faith. All those who follow Jesus will stand at the crossroads of fear on many occasions. The key is that we turn to God and not away from him at these moments.

THE PRAYER
of a Leader

As you prepare to lead this small group, take time to examine your heart and life. Are there places where anxiety and fear have control? Maybe you have faced a conflict with someone and it is causing you to worry. Possibly you have received some bad news recently. Lay any area of anxiety you are facing before God in prayer and ask him to help you learn to walk in deeper levels of trust.

Question 1

As we read the Old Testament, it becomes apparent that the nations all around Canaan had a hard time getting along with each other. Each one was trying to build its own empire. In most cases the process of empire-building was not about national honor. The primary driving force behind empire-building was economic prosperity and survival.

All nations have to face the reality of debt and economic problems at some point in their history. In those days the kings would build palaces, roads, and other projects. They also had to maintain a military for the protection of their cities. There was no banking system, so that no loans could be negotiated for all they wanted to do. Thus, the kings of these nations would invade and take over a neighboring country. This was instant income!

Not only would their invasion and conquering of another people group get instant wealth, but it would also provide an ongoing source of revenue for years to come. Once they ruled a nation, they would force them to pay regular tribute or taxes. The process of empire-building and expansion was motivated by the desire for wealth more than anything else.

THE RISE OF ASSYRIA

One reason why Israel was able to exist as a nation for many centuries was that there were no dominant superpowers in their region for much of their history. There were superpowers in the ancient world, such as Egypt, Assyria, Babylonia, and Persia. But for several centuries, all of them were essentially dormant. Then around 750 B.C., Assyria began its ascendancy. It started taking over smaller countries all around Israel. As they took over a country, they sought to leave behind the smallest occupational force possible. The goal was to retain control of the region, but not weaken their military force in the process by spreading themselves too thin. They wanted their army to be able to fight new battles and conquer other countries.

What Assyria (and other ancient nations) learned was that if they conquered a country and left a small force occupying the land, with time the people would revolt. To counteract this threat, they began sending thousands of conquered people into exile and replacing them with people from other nations. After this population shift, it took a much smaller occupational army to maintain control of a region because the people lost their sense of national identity. This is exactly what happened to Israel (the northern kingdom) in 712 B.C.

Questions 2–4

In Isaiah 7 we read that Assyria is on the march. They are in a process of empire-building and are swallowing up small countries all around Canaan. These small countries realize that they are vulnerable, so some of them begin to look for possible military alliances. Israel (the northern kingdom) and Aram form an alliance in order to resist the Assyrian army. They come to Ahaz, the king of Judah, and invite him to join their alliance.

For the sake of self-preservation, one would think Ahaz would say yes. But Ahaz says, "No." He wants nothing to do with a battle against Assyria.

Thus, the kings of Israel and Aram decide to go to war against Ahaz (and Judah). Their hope is to conquer Judah and force them to stand with them against the imminent Assyrian invasion. When Ahaz hears that Israel and Aram have formed an alliance and are coming against his nation, we read these words: "The hearts of Ahaz and his people were shaken, as the trees of the forest are shaken by the wind" (Isaiah 7:2).

What a vivid picture! Ahaz and the people of Judah feel trapped. Assyria is on the march. Israel and Aram are plotting against them. They

LEADER'S NOTES

are trembling like trees of the forest when the winds blow! They are shaking in their boots. Isaiah paints a colorful picture of the anxiety and fear that have gripped the heart of Ahaz and Judah.

The question of the hour becomes, *Where will Ahaz and Judah turn in this desperate hour?* They don't want to throw their lot in with Israel and Aram. They know Assyria is too powerful for them to handle. Where will they turn?

Isaiah knows what temptation faces Ahaz. The prophet knows that Ahaz will soon be contemplating an unthinkable option. Ahaz will soon be considering an alliance with Assyria. Since the Assyrians are the rising superpower, an alliance with them will grant protection from their invasion and a guarantee that Israel and Aram will back off.

To Ahaz, forming an alliance seems like a good idea. But this is not God's plan for the nation of Judah. God is about to use Assyria to bring judgment on the northern kingdom—on Israel—because of their unfaithfulness and their treatment of the poor. But Assyria will also be coming under judgment because of their idolatry, corruption, violence, and paganism. God does not want Judah in partnership with either of these nations. Their company is bad company! To partner with them is to enter into their rebellion and sin. It also means taking the possible risk of coming under their judgment.

What God wants is for his people to place their trust in him. Rather than running to the new superpower or bowing to the pressure of neighboring nations, God longs for his people to place their trust in his ability to save them.

Ahaz reveals something that is deeply rooted in human nature. We'd like to do right, but we also want to keep our options open. We often try to keep an escape route, even though we may know God will not approve of it. We'd like to be honest, but if we find ourselves in a desperate situation, we are ready to lie if we have to.

God wants to reveal his presence and power and invite us into a life of full devotion. We tend to prefer convenient and limited levels of devotion that allow us to keep a few options on the back burner just in case.

Questions 5–7

This is called psychological warfare! The commander of Assyria is intentionally speaking to all the people on the wall in their language. He wants the word spread through Jerusalem. He knows that in a matter of hours rumors will be spreading all over the city—rumors such as, "Hezekiah is deceiving us; God can't get us out of this situation. We will all die of starvation when Assyria lays siege to the city. There is no way we can resist the army of Assyria; we are as good as defeated already."

The Assyrians know that once the people are gripped by fear, their faith, loyalty, and unity will be gone. They know that fear will destroy confidence, paralyze the people, and turn them against each other. What is true then about the power of fear is still true today.

Fear is the great enemy of spiritual community. Every time we choose fear over self-disclosure or being known, we paralyze community. Each time we choose fear over a needed confrontation, we weaken the fabric of Christian community. Every time we bow to fear and refuse to speak the truth in love, community dies a little.

Building a healthy community really does require boldness and fearlessness. In Isaiah 37, the prophet comes to Hezekiah to encourage him to respond in a God-honoring way to the threats he is facing. Isaiah has seen kings come and go. He saw Ahaz give in to fear and live with staggering consequences. But he tells Hezekiah the same thing he told Ahaz: "Trust God. Be brave. Stand strong in your faith."

The good news is that Hezekiah listens and follows the wise counsel of Isaiah. He doesn't surrender to Assyria. He stands firm in his faith. No matter what the odds, threats, or possible repercussions, Hezekiah commits to following God and not a human being.

Word of Hezekiah's bold refusal to bow to the might of Assyria gets back to Sennacherib, the king of Assyria. He hears that Judah is defying him and Hezekiah is trusting in God rather than him. We can be confident that Sennacherib is outraged! He sits down and writes Hezekiah a letter.

We must remember that there were no telegrams or emails in those days. When communication happened, it could take days or weeks. Hezekiah and the people of Israel would be waiting to hear how Sennacherib will respond to Hezekiah's defiance.

They wait, and wait, and wait some more. Then, all of a sudden, Hezekiah gets a letter signed by the king of Assyria:

> *Say to Hezekiah king of Judah: Do not let the god you depend on deceive you when he says, "Jerusalem will not be handed over to the king of Assyria." Surely you have heard what the kings of Assyria have done to all the countries, destroying them completely. And will you be delivered? Did the gods of the nations that were destroyed by my forefathers deliver them?" (Isaiah 37:10–12)*

The king of Assyria then runs through a laundry list of other countries that have been defeated by his army. This is the worst news possible for Judah and Hezekiah. Sennacherib is saying, "I will completely destroy you and your puny little nation. I've done it before, and I will do it again." Humanly speaking, Sennacherib is absolutely right, the impending battle between Judah and the might of Assyria is no contest.

THE THREAT OF A SIEGE

Assyria has a military strategy that has been employed by many before them. It is called a siege. We know that this is their plan of attack against Judah because of the words of the Assyrian commander: "Was it only to your master and you that my master sent me to say these things, and not to the men sitting on the wall—who, like you, will have to eat their own filth and drink their own urine?" (Isaiah 36:12).

He wants the people to know, in their own language, what lies ahead if they defy the king and army of Assyria. The comment about eating their own filth and drinking their own urine is not meant to be some kind of disgusting word picture. It is a threat of siege.

In those days, one form of warfare was to surround a city and simply wait until the people were starving to death. At some point, when the conditions became bad enough, the people in the city would surrender. Throughout ancient history the people trapped in a city during a siege were driven to a point of desperation where they even considered cannibalism to stay alive (see Lamentations 2:11–12, 19–20). The commander of Assyria is telling the people, "You had better hear what I say because you will also come to a place of utter starvation if you refuse to obey the king of Assyria. We will wait it out as long as it takes."

Questions 8-9

The angel of God comes and completely routs the Assyrian army, and they go home. From this point on in history, Assyria goes into a decline from which it never recovers.

As we look back on this biblical account, we realize that Hezekiah was never really alone. He faced hard times and his faith was tested, but God was with him every step of the way. Just as God was with Hezekiah, he wants to be with us. God wants us to avoid the pitfalls of Ahaz. We don't have to live under the tyranny of fear and anxiety. We are called to lives of trust and faith.

All of us have ups and downs. No matter how much we love God and walk with Jesus, we still have moments when anxiety slips in. But, through the power of God's Holy Spirit, we can have lives that are predominantly characterized by the peace and freedom that come from God's presence in our lives. That's how God wants us to live.

Micah: Doing Justice

THE HEART
of a Leader

The prophets are deeply concerned that followers of God do not fall into the trap of "being religious" and at the same time fail to have a heart that reflects the concerns of God. As you prepare to lead this small group, take time for self-examination. How can you live in a way that brings God's justice alive in this world? Is your heart tender toward others and do you show kindness freely? How can you grow in humility? Also, take time to think about your habits as a worshiper. Are you just going through the motions, or are you truly meeting God in worship? Does worship bring transforming power into your life?

THE PRAYER
of a Leader

Meditate on Micah 6:8 as part of your preparation for leading your small group. Ask God to help you grow in justice, mercy, and humility.

Question 1

We are often numb and don't notice the sin around us. The prophets, by contrast, act as if the world is falling apart. They suggest that these things are a much bigger deal than we ever thought. They are echoing the heart of God, who sees and cares about all of these things. All of these things are a bigger deal than we would have ever guessed! Every time we read the prophets, we get a bucket of ice-cold water poured over our head and an ear-piercing, "Wake up!"

Questions 2–4

All through the Old Testament we get a window into the heart of the prophets. From some of their words, it would be easy to get the feeling that the prophets got up on the wrong side of the bed. Amos calls the women of Israel cows. Ouch! He is saying that they are more concerned about where they will get their next drink than about the poor and the needy. Isaiah tells the people that God is fed up with their offerings, gatherings, and religious lives. Their injustice trumps their religious

LEADER'S NOTES

activities and makes God sick! Micah uses gory and graphic metaphors, but his message is loud and clear. The people are filled with injustice and the consequences are grave.

Let's be honest, it is easy to avoid reading the prophets. As a matter of fact, many people do exactly that. The prophets hold a mirror up to our souls and show us where we have become marred, scarred, and ugly. They are not really happy books. They tell us things we don't want to hear. They convict us of sin. They remind us that there are serious consequences for rebelling against God. It is easy to avoid and relegate these words to some kind of secondary status.

If we fall for the temptation to avoid reading the prophets, we do so to our own peril. We need the message they bring. We need the manner in which they communicate. Sometimes a gentle reminder does not get our attention and a spiritual two-by-four is needed to wake us up!

The voice of Jesus enters in with the voices of the prophets. He also reminds us that God is concerned about justice and righteousness. Note his words in Matthew 25:34–36:

> Then the King will say to those on his right, "Come, you who are blessed by my Father; take your inheritance, the kingdom prepared for you since the creation of the world. For I was hungry and you gave me something to eat, I was thirsty and you gave me something to drink, I was a stranger and you invited me in, I needed clothes and you clothed me, I was sick and you looked after me, I was in prison and you came to visit me."

If we ever wonder whether the prophets are overstating their case, all we have to do is read these words of Jesus. He is clear that justice and righteousness matter more than we dream.

Questions 5–7

Prophet after prophet teach the same lesson. People don't really want to know the truth about sin and what it has done to our lives, society, and the world. Hearing the voice of the prophets and seeing the broken heart of God make us uncomfortable. It is easier to live with blind eyes, deaf ears, and a hard heart.

Time and time again through the Old Testament the prophets come with stern warnings from God. They come to help the people see, hear, and feel with God. Over and over the people reject these prophets. Sometimes the people laugh, at other times they mock, and still other times they simply walk away. Sadly, there are also times when the people lash out in anger. Prophets are then beaten, imprisoned, and even killed!

Today the response to the prophets tends to be a little tamer. Most people simply avoid them. The voices of the prophets still cry out. They still help to pierce our hearts with the truth of God. Will we fight and resist, or will we receive the words of the prophets with humility?

Events that horrified the prophets have become everyday occurrences in our world. Things that the prophets condemned in the name of God have become standard business practice and normal operating procedures in the marketplace today. Attitudes that brought condemnation from the prophets are tolerated in our society and often in our local churches. We have become so comfortable and complacent that we hardly notice the presence of sin around us.

It is like a necklace or ring that feels strange when we first put it on. After a short time, we don't even notice it. Or it is like a broken item around the house. It bugs us at first, but with time, it just blends in. We don't even see it anymore. With time, things that should bother us and break our hearts can become part of the landscape of our lives. The job of the prophets is to get our attention and help us notice what we have forgotten.

Questions 8–9

What God wants is us! He wants our hearts and lives fully yielded to him. What God asks for is something anyone can give. He wants us to act in ways that reflect his justice. He invites us to love that which is merciful. Moreover, God wants us to walk in authentic humility with him. If we are humble before God, we will follow him and our whole life will be his. This is what God wants from each of his children.

God loves worship, but only if it comes from a life that seeks justice, mercy, and humility. Once we begin to respond to the leading of the Holy Spirit through the conviction of the prophets, our worship makes sense. Once God has our hearts, the way we use our resources adjusts to reflect the desires of the God who gives us all that we have. When justice is pouring through our lives, relationships are filled with love and compassion. This is God's vision for his children:

> He has showed you, O man, what is good.
> And what does the LORD require of you?
> To act justly and to love mercy
> and to walk humbly with your God. (Micah 6:8)

LEADER'S NOTES

THE HEART
of a Leader

Every follower of Christ will experience moments of struggle and pain. We can be right in the center of God's will, and it may be a hard place. Take time to reflect on your past. How have you experienced God's presence, care, and strength revealed in the midst of a hard time? When have you been obedient to God's call and discovered that it was a hard place to be? You may even be in such a place right now. Search your heart and ask God to help you see that his call is always right, even when it is difficult.

THE PRAYER
of a Leader

Ask God to help you communicate with humble honesty. Some of your small group members may be in the midst of a painful time. They may be walking the road that Jeremiah walked. Ask God to prepare your heart as you lead this study that unveils the truth that being in God's will does not mean a painless existence. Also pray that God will use you to help people see that hard assignments can bring them closer to God.

Questions 2-3 Jer. 1:4-10, 17-19

God's call to Jeremiah was loud and clear. Anyone who wonders whether Jeremiah is on the right track has failed to read his story. God lets Jeremiah know that his call came from the first moment of his conception:

> Before I formed you in the womb I knew you,
> before you were born I set you apart;
> I appointed you as a prophet to the nations. (Jeremiah 1:5)

Jeremiah, like many of us, has a sense that he is not up to the task God has placed before him. He has a healthy understanding of his own frailness and wonders whether he can fulfill God's plan for his life. He cries out, "Ah, Sovereign LORD, I do not know how to speak; I am only a child" (Jeremiah 1:6).

God reassures Jeremiah and lets him know that his abilities and strength are not the primary issue. His job is to follow God's leading and speak the words God has called him to proclaim. God responds to Jeremiah: "Do not say, 'I am only a child.' You must go to everyone I send you to and say whatever I command you. Do not be afraid of them, for I am with you and will rescue you..." (Jeremiah 1:7–8).

Finally, God gives Jeremiah a hint of what lies ahead in his ministry. When we read these words, we get a sense that Jeremiah is not heading out on a journey that will be smooth and easy:

> *Get yourself ready! Stand up and say to them whatever I command you. Do not be terrified by them, or I will terrify you before them. Today I have made you a fortified city, an iron pillar and a bronze wall to stand against the whole land—against the kings of Judah, its officials, its priests and the people of the land. They will fight against you but will not overcome you, for I am with you and will rescue you....* (Jeremiah 1:17–19)

In Jeremiah 2–19, the prophet speaks the words of God. He is faithful to his calling, doing the work God wants him to do. Sadly, the people don't respond the way Jeremiah hopes. They are clearly resistant to his messages. Like any communicator, Jeremiah longs for the people to hear, be touched, and respond. Yet Jeremiah's words seem to be hitting deaf ears and hard hearts.

Thus, in chapter 19, God calls Jeremiah to turn up the heat. He gives him an illustration, a picture to help the people get the point. Jeremiah buys a jar, under the direction of God, and uses it to show them what is coming if they don't repent and turn from their wicked ways. He stands in front of all the leaders of the nation of Judah, and says, "I'm telling you one last time, 'Humble yourself before God. Stop worshiping foreign gods. Reduce your pride. Open your hearts to his leading and promptings.' And if you don't... watch closely now!" Then, Jeremiah smashes the jar.

Questions 4–5   Jer. 20: 1-2, 7-8; 37:15-16, 20

As we read Jeremiah 20–37, the faithful prophet goes out and speaks God's words again and again. The fire that burns in him propels him through beatings, rejection, and discouragement out into ministry again. We find ourselves hoping that this time the people will respond. Maybe they will see Jeremiah's courage and listen to the words God is speaking through him. Maybe this time they will get the message. Maybe the lesson of the broken clay jar will sink in and the people will respond.

Sadly, the opposite happens. Jeremiah is beaten again and then thrown into a dungeon for "a long time" (Jeremiah 37:15–16). This ministry to which God has called Jeremiah is hard and getting harder. Jeremiah, for the life of him, cannot figure out why things are turning out this way. This is not what he signed up for. This is not how he thought it was going to turn out. He actually comes to the point that he feels if he stays imprisoned, he will die (Jeremiah 37:20).

Jeremiah, remarkably, continues to speak the words of God after two beatings, being put in stocks, and being thrown into a dungeon. In response to his continued ministry and preaching, Jeremiah is thrown into a cistern. We read that he is lowered with a rope into a cistern filled with mud. His enemies plan on leaving him there until he dies (Jeremiah 38:7–9).

Later, when Jeremiah's friends find out that he's been put in that cistern, they bargain for his release. With time, they are able to pull him out with ropes, clean him up, and set him free. Take a wild guess at what Jeremiah does when he is released from his death sentence in the cistern. He goes right back out again to declare the words of God to the people who have resisted and rejected him over and over before!

Questions 6–7

When you know the story of Jeremiah, you begin to understand why he is nicknamed "The Weeping Prophet." Later in life, after the fall of Jerusalem, Jeremiah writes the book of Lamentations—a reflection on how God feels about what happened to Jerusalem and his people. It also expresses the heart of Jeremiah, the man who did all he could to call the people to repent so that they would not have to face the invasion of Babylon and the destruction of the holy city.

In the book of Ecclesiastes we are told that there is a time for everything. The writer says there is, among other things:

> a time to weep and a time to laugh,
> a time to mourn and a time to dance. (Ecclesiastes 3:4)

Jeremiah has learned that tears are often appropriate. In particular, when the heart of God is broken, our hearts should break as well. When we see people who resist God and run from his grace, we should be sad, even as God is sad. When we see sin in our lives, tears are appropriate; and these tears should lead to change! Jeremiah teaches us that there are times when tears and mourning are the right response.

Those who have received a difficult assignment from God need to pull up a chair at the feet of Jeremiah. From the vantage point of the casual observer, Jeremiah's whole ministry seems like a total bust. He has preached his heart out for four decades, and *nobody ever responded*. He has warned, pleaded, prayed, and smashed jars, and *no one repented*. Jeremiah's ministry never went the way that he had envisioned. Yet he wept, looked back to God, and continued on.

LEADER'S NOTES

JER. 20:7-8

Questions 8-10

Jeremiah is not afraid to tell God how he feels about all he is facing. He feels tricked, deceived, discouraged, and beaten up. The fresh-faced young buck who ran so hard at the start of his ministry has become tired and worn out.

Yet, from the depths of his pain and sorrow, Jeremiah's heart shows through. Although he has been beaten, rejected, mocked, scorned, and openly humiliated, he is still ready to follow the God who formed him in his mother's womb and called him from his childhood.

Jeremiah says, "Even if I wanted to stop speaking for God, I can't! His truth is like a fire burning in my soul. I must speak for God! I must do my ministry. I will press on." What an example of tenacious faithfulness in the furnace of life.

Jeremiah presses on in ministry, but he also expresses all that is on his heart. He prays to God with a purity, passion, and brutal honesty not often paralleled in the Scriptures or in prayers today. Here are some of the components of Jeremiah's prayer:

- *Jeremiah accuses God of tricking him.* He says, "You deceived me" (Jeremiah 20:7). The root word used here means that Jeremiah feels seduced under false pretenses. He tells God that things are not turning out as he thought they would. Jeremiah pours out honest frustration.
- *Jeremiah tells God that his life and ministry don't make sense.* He lets God know that he does not understand why things are going so wrong when he is doing what God commanded (Jeremiah 20:7–8).
- *Jeremiah curses the day he was born.* Just like Job, Jeremiah curses the fact that he was born (Jeremiah 20:14–15). Job is saying, "I hate my birthday!" He even goes so far as to say, "I hate the guy who burst out of the room with cigars saying, 'It's a boy!'"

Yet Jeremiah does what all of us can do. He hangs in there! He is bruised, battered, and discouraged, but he keeps his eyes on God. He expresses his sorrow and confusion, but he keeps on preaching. He is knocked down, but he gets up again.

Ordinary people can stand strong even when it hurts. If you were to talk with a dozen followers of Christ who have stood fast during a hard time, through tears and suffering, you will find a common theme. Each one will tell you that they are glad they hung in there. They are thankful that they did not throw in the towel and quit. In the same way,

> **It isn't what you wish to do, it's what you will do for God that transforms your life.**
>
> HENRIETTA C. MEARS

if you ask those who have faced hard times in their faith and have caved in to pressure, they will tell you how much they regret it.

Jeremiah teaches us another lesson as we look at his life. In his prayer that is recorded in chapter 20, he expresses deep pain and frustration. Yet, right in the middle of his prayer, we are surprised with these words:

> Sing to the LORD!
> Give praise to the LORD!
> He rescues the life of the needy
> from the hands of the wicked. (Jeremiah 20:13)

These words come out of nowhere. Jeremiah is experiencing the worst time of his life. He is pouring his heart out in a messy prayer—and he starts praising God.

The Life-Giving Power of Hope

THE HEART
of a Leader

God breathes hope. All through the Old Testament, even in the most painful and darkest moments of Israel's history, God loves and leads his people. From the harshest moments of judgment, we can hear the message of hope come through.

Take time as a leader and think through your own reading of the Old Testament. How have you seen God show up among his people and bring hope? How have you experienced God's hope filling your life during the Old Testament Challenge? How has a new hope in God and love for his Word grown in your small group?

THE PRAYER
of a Leader

As you reflect on the hope-filled moments you have experienced as a small group, celebrate God's goodness and let this spirit of confidence in God's power and love guide your teaching of this final small group session. Pray for hope to fill each of your small group members. If you know of specific people who are facing hard times, pray specifically for them to be surprised by the hope of God as you walk through this study.

Question 1

Everyone has certain moments in their personal history that are low points. This is also true of nations. For God's people, one of the saddest moments came in 586 B.C., when Nebuchadnezzar and the armies of Babylon invaded Jerusalem and conquered it. They had come before and placed the people of Judah under their control, but they had always left the nation intact and someone on the throne. In 586 B.C. they exiled the people and destroyed the city. It was the saddest day in the history of Israel.

Back in 722 B.C. the Assyrians had conquered the northern kingdom. At that time, ten of the twelve tribes of God's people had ceased to exist. Then, in 586 B.C. the southern kingdom fell. This marked the end of Israel as a nation with their own God-appointed leader. They were no longer a united nation, or a divided nation—they were exiled!

LEADER'S NOTES

LEADER'S NOTES

Questions 2–3

In 2 Kings 25 we get a picture of how bad things got near the end of Judah's history. Babylon had become the dominant world power. Jeremiah, who was a prophet at that time, kept saying to people, "Exile is coming. Babylon will invade and conquer Jerusalem." But the people would not believe him. They were sure God would never let the holy city of Jerusalem fall under the sword of a foreign army.

Sadly, everything Jeremiah predicted came true. Zedekiah, one of the final kings of Judah, rebelled against the king of Babylon. As a punishment, Zedekiah's sons were murdered in front of him and then his eyes were gouged out so that this would be the last thing he ever saw. Nebuchadnezzar set the temple of God on fire, destroyed the palace and every important building in Jerusalem, and finally broke down the wall of the city. It was a complete and utter conquest of the capital of the nation of Judah and subjugation of all those with any political power.

Those who were not killed were exiled to Babylon. A handful of the poorest of the land were left to tend any part of the land that could be productive. Even this small group was under the hand of Babylon and was forced to pay tribute to the king.

Imagine, for a moment, that you were forced to leave everything familiar. You have to leave your home and your country and go live in a place that you don't know. You lose your job. You don't know the local language but are forced to learn it. You don't know the customs. Everything is different.

Once you arrive as a prisoner of war in your new country, you realize that you will never have power in this place. You will never have influence. You have no resources, no wealth, and no means of attaining them. You are a stranger in a strange land. You will never belong. Your children will grow up with no connection to their national or religious roots except what you try to pass on to them. That's what it meant for people of Judah to live in exile. It looked like the end of the dream.

Questions 4–5

If we were in Jeremiah's shoes, what phrase do you think we might be tempted to use at the beginning of a letter to the people in exile? Jeremiah had been giving them warnings for years, but they had ignored him! They had been given countless chances to repent and turn around, but they refused! Jeremiah spoke the truth again and again, only to be met with resistance, beatings, and rejection. After all of this, when judgment finally came and everything Jeremiah prophesied came to pass, what four words could Jeremiah have used to start his letter? It would have been easy for Jeremiah to say, "I told you so!" But, he does not.

Questions 6-7

At the beginning of the Old Testament Challenge, when we studied the desert wanderings of Israel, we learned that God cared more about who his people were becoming than he did about how long it took them to arrive in the Promised Land. Again we see that God is shaping his people. He intends to bring them back home, but he wants them to experience growth in their seventy years of captivity. Jeremiah lets the people know that this captivity does not mean the end of their people, culture, and faith. In seventy years they will have another chance to realize God's dream of building a new community of people who love and follow him.

When God calls the people to pray for God's blessing on Babylon, this should be a familiar theme to followers of Christ. It was Jesus who said:

> You have heard that it was said, "Love your neighbor and hate your enemy." But I tell you: Love your enemies and pray for those who persecute you, that you may be sons of your Father in heaven. He causes his sun to rise on the evil and the good, and sends rain on the righteous and the unrighteous. (Matthew 5:43–45)

The heart of God, in both the Old and New Testaments, beats with love. He wants us, as his children, to operate with compassion and mercy, even toward those who have wronged us.

GOD'S HAND IN HISTORY

By every known law of human history, the people of Israel should have ceased to exist after 586 B.C. There is no way on earth the people of Israel should have survived, except for one thing: God chose that they would. God chose it.

After Nebuchadnezzar died in 562 B.C., Babylon went into rapid decline. It was invaded and defeated by a new kingdom—Persia. Cyrus, the king of Persia, decided on a new way to handle exiled people. Under the hand of God, he released the people and allowed them to go back to their homeland.

The behavior of Cyrus was unprecedented in the ancient world. His choice came because "the LORD moved his heart." What a reminder that God's hand is always active in human history. We don't know if Cyrus had any idea that God was working, but through his life, God spared his people and brought them home. On top of it all, Cyrus even did some fund-raising and helped gather resources so that God's people could go back to Jerusalem and begin reconstruction of their city and temple.

LEADER'S NOTES

Questions 8–10

From the very beginning of God's interaction with human beings, he was waiting for a group of people willing to form a community and say, "God, not our will, but yours be done." He longed to see his followers live lives that declared, "We will die to all the stupid, foolish dreams of our lives. We will not long for and invest our lives in the pursuit of wealth, power, and success. We will long for your will, and your will alone."

The irony with Israel is that when they had a place of authority and power, they never used it to expand God's kingdom. When they had kings on the throne with all their military might, they seemed to become weaker and weaker. Now, with no formal government, no army, no wealth, most of their population gone, and no human authority at all, they finally come to a place where God can use them. They are finally ready to say, "Not our will, but yours be done!"

LEADER'S NOTES

WILLOW
Willow Creek Association

Willow Creek Association
Vision, Training, Resources for Prevailing Churches

This resource was created to serve you and to help you in building a local church that prevails!

Since 1992, the Willow Creek Association (WCA) has been linking like-minded, action-oriented churches with each other and with strategic vision, training, and resources. Now a worldwide network of over 6,400 churches from more than ninety denominations, the WCA works to equip Member Churches and others with the tools needed to build prevailing churches. Our desire is to inspire, equip, and encourage Christian leaders to build biblically functioning churches that reach increasing numbers of unchurched people, not just with innovations from Willow Creek Community Church in South Barrington, Illinois, but from any church in the world that has experienced God-given breakthroughs.

WILLOW CREEK CONFERENCES
Each year, thousands of local church leaders, staff and volunteers—from WCA Member Churches and others—attend one of our conferences or training events. Conferences offered on the Willow Creek campus in South Barrington, Illinois, include:

Prevailing Church Conference: Foundational training for staff and volunteers working to build a prevailing local church.

Prevailing Church Workshops: More than fifty strategic, day-long workshops covering seven topic areas that represent key characteristics of a prevailing church; offered twice each year.

Promiseland Conference: Children's ministries; infant through fifth grade.

Student Ministries Conference: Junior and senior high ministries.

Willow Creek Arts Conference: Vision and training for Christian artists using their gifts in the ministries of local churches.

Leadership Summit: Envisioning and equipping Christians with leadership gifts and respon-sibilities; broadcast live via satellite to eighteen cities across North America.

Contagious Evangelism Conference: Encouragement and training for churches and church leaders who want to be strategic in reaching lost people for Christ.

Small Groups Conference: Exploring how developing a church *of* small groups can play a vital role in developing authentic Christian community that leads to spiritual transformation.

To find out more about WCA conferences, visit our website at www.willowcreek.com.

PREVAILING CHURCH REGIONAL WORKSHOPS
Each year the WCA team leads several, two-day training events in select cities across the United States. Some twenty day-long workshops are offered in topic areas including leadership, next-

generation ministries, small groups, arts and worship, evangelism, spiritual gifts, financial stewardship, and spiritual formation. These events make quality training more accessible and affordable to larger groups of staff and volunteers.

To find out more about Prevailing Church Regional Workshops, visit our website at www.willowcreek.com.

WILLOW CREEK RESOURCES™

Churches can look to Willow Creek Resources™ for a trusted channel of ministry tools in areas of leadership, evangelism, spiritual gifts, small groups, drama, contemporary music, financial stewardship, spiritual transformation, and more. For ordering information, call (800) 570-9812 or visit our website at www.willowcreek.com.

WCA MEMBERSHIP

Membership in the Willow Creek Association as well as attendance at WCA Conferences is for churches, ministries, and leaders who hold to a historic, orthodox understanding of biblical Christianity. The annual church membership fee of $249 provides substantial discounts for your entire team on all conferences and Willow Creek Resources, networking opportunities with other outreach-oriented churches, a bimonthly newsletter, a subscription to the *Defining Moments* monthly audio journal for leaders, and more.

To find out more about WCA membership, visit our website at www.willowcreek.com.

WILLOWNET (WWW.WILLOWCREEK.COM)

This Internet resource service provides access to hundreds of Willow Creek messages, drama scripts, songs, videos, and multimedia ideas. The system allows you to sort through these elements and download them for a fee.

Our website also provides detailed information on the Willow Creek Association, Willow Creek Community Church, WCA membership, conferences, training events, resources, and more.

WILLOWCHARTS.COM (WWW.WILLOWCHARTS.COM)

Designed for local church worship leaders and musicians, WillowCharts.com provides online access to hundreds of music charts and chart components, including choir, orchestral, and horn sections, as well as rehearsal tracks and video streaming of Willow Creek Community Church performances.

THE NET (HTTP://STUDENTMINISTRY.WILLOWCREEK.COM)

The NET is an online training and resource center designed by and for student ministry leaders. It provides an inside look at the structure, vision, and mission of prevailing student ministries from around the world. The NET gives leaders access to complete programming elements, including message outlines, dramas, small group questions, and more. An indispensable resource and networking tool for prevailing student ministry leaders!

CONTACT THE WILLOW CREEK ASSOCIATION

If you have comments or questions, or would like to find out more about WCA events or resources, please contact us:

Willow Creek Association
P.O. Box 3188, Barrington, IL 60011-3188
Phone: (800) 570-9812 or (847) 765-0070
Fax: (888) 922-0035 or (847) 765-5046
Web: www.willowcreek.com